AF316790

FORBIDDEN FREQUENCIES

FORBIDDEN FREQUENCIES

Unveiling the World's Hidden Truths

DEMETRI WELSH

www.demetriwelsh.com

Contents

INTRODUCTION TO PART FOUR
GOVERNMENT COVER-UPS AND MODERN CONSPIRACIES

INTRODUCTION TO PART FIVE
THE POWER OF BELIEF AND THE PERSISTENCE OF MYSTERY

EPILOGUE
EMBRACING THE UNKNOWN

To those who dare to question,

This book is dedicated to the seekers, the rebels, and the truth-tellers. To those who look beyond the surface, who refuse to accept the world as it is presented, and who strive to uncover the hidden layers of reality.

To my family and friends, thank you for your unwavering support and encouragement throughout this journey. Your belief in my vision has been a constant source of strength.

And to my listeners and readers, who share in the pursuit of forbidden knowledge, this book is for you. May it inspire you to continue exploring the unknown, challenging the status quo, and seeking the truths that lie beyond the veil.

— Demetri Welsh

Prologue

Greetings, fellow seekers of truth. I'm Demetri Welsh, and I invite you to embark on a journey into the realms of the forbidden, the hidden, and the controversial. Welcome to *Forbidden FREQUENCIES: Unveiling the World's Hidden Truths*.

From an early age, I was captivated by the mysteries that our world holds. The tales of ancient civilizations, the whispers of secret societies, and the enigmatic symbols scattered throughout history intrigued me. As I delved deeper into these mysteries, I realized that much of what we are told is merely the surface of a much deeper and darker reality.

In our modern world, information is more accessible than ever, yet the most profound truths remain buried, obscured by layers of disinformation, secrecy, and manipulation. Governments, religious institutions, and powerful elites have long kept a tight grip on knowledge that could challenge the very foundations of our understanding. This book is my attempt to peel back those layers and reveal the truths that lie beneath.

Why Forbidden Knowledge?

The term "forbidden knowledge" refers to information that has been deliberately concealed from the public, often because it threatens established power structures or challenges widely accepted beliefs. Throughout history, those who sought such knowledge were often labeled heretics, blasphemers, or conspiracy theorists. But it is precisely this type of knowledge that has the power to awaken, to enlighten, and to transform.

In these pages, you will find an exploration of some of the most controversial and provocative topics imaginable. We will journey through the lost civilizations of Atlantis and ancient Egypt, uncover the esoteric teachings of the Gnostics and alchemists, and delve into the shadowy world of secret societies like the Freemasons and the Illuminati. We will examine the evidence of extraterrestrial influence on our planet, from ancient astronaut theories to modern UFO sightings. And we will expose government cover-ups and modern conspiracies that continue to shape our world today.

Setting the Tone

This book is not for the faint of heart. It is unfiltered and raw, embracing adult themes and controversial viewpoints. My aim is to provoke thought, to challenge assumptions, and to inspire you to seek your own truths. The journey we are about to undertake is as much about questioning the known as it is about discovering the unknown.

A Personal Journey

My own path to understanding has been unconventional, to say the least. As a psychic reader and energy worker, I have spent years navigating the unseen realms of existence. My work has brought me into contact with individuals from all walks of life, each with their own stories and secrets. Through my podcast, *Forbidden Frequencies*, I have had the privilege of sharing these stories and exploring these mysteries with a wider audience.

This book represents the culmination of my experiences and insights. It is a synthesis of my research, my encounters, and my reflections on the forbidden knowledge that has shaped our world. It is my hope that, through these pages, you too will be inspired to question, to seek, and to discover.

What to Expect

Each chapter of this book is a deep dive into a different aspect of forbidden knowledge. We will begin with ancient mysteries and lost civilizations, move on to occult practices and esoteric teachings, and then explore the hidden agendas of secret societies and the truths behind extraterrestrial connections. We will conclude with an examination of modern conspiracies and government cover-ups, tying together the threads of our investigation.

Along the way, I will share my personal insights and controversial opinions, drawing on both historical evidence and contemporary accounts. Interspersed throughout the chapters are thought-provoking questions and statements designed to keep you engaged and questioning.

A Word of Caution

The topics covered in this book are highly controversial and may challenge your existing beliefs. Some of the material may be disturbing or unsettling. I urge you to approach these pages with an open mind and a critical eye. The truth, as they say, is often stranger than fiction.

Conclusion

As we embark on this journey together, I encourage you to embrace the spirit of inquiry. Let us delve into the unknown, question the unquestionable, and seek the forbidden frequencies that resonate just beneath the surface of our reality.

Welcome to *Forbidden FREQUENCIES: Unveiling the World's Hidden Truths*. The journey begins now.

— Demetri Welsh

INTRODUCTION TO PART ONE

Ancient Mysteries and Lost Civilizations

Throughout history, the world has been home to civilizations that have risen and fallen, leaving behind enigmatic traces of their existence. These ancient cultures, shrouded in mystery and intrigue, have captivated the imaginations of scholars, adventurers, and truth-seekers for centuries. From the lost city of Atlantis to the pyramids of Egypt, these remnants of bygone eras beckon us to uncover their secrets and understand the true nature of our past.

Part One of *Forbidden FREQUENCIES: Unveiling the World's Hidden Truths* is dedicated to exploring these ancient mysteries and lost civilizations. We will delve into the stories and theories that surround these enigmatic cultures, examining the evidence that challenges conventional historical narratives. Our journey will take us to the depths of the ocean, the heart of the desert, and the peaks of forgotten mountains, as we seek to uncover the hidden truths that lie buried beneath the sands of time.

The Enigma of Atlantis

Our journey begins with Atlantis, the legendary island nation described by the ancient Greek philosopher Plato. According to Plato, Atlantis was a powerful and technologically advanced civilization that existed thousands of years before his time. Its sudden disappearance, engulfed by the sea, has fueled countless theories and speculations. Was Atlantis a real place, or merely a myth? If it did exist, what caused its catastrophic demise? We will examine the evidence and explore the various hypotheses that have been proposed, from natural disasters to extraterrestrial intervention.

The Mysteries of Egypt

Next, we will venture to the land of the pharaohs, where the pyramids of Giza stand as silent sentinels of an ancient and advanced civilization. The construction techniques used to build these monumental structures remain a subject of debate among historians and engineers. Were they built by human hands alone, or did the ancient Egyptians possess knowledge and technology far beyond our own? We will also explore the Sphinx, a colossal statue whose true age and purpose continue to elude scholars.

South American Enigmas

Our exploration will then take us to South America, where the Nazca Lines stretch across the Peruvian desert. These massive geoglyphs, visible only from the air, have puzzled researchers since their discovery. Were they created as messages to the gods, astronomical calendars, or landing strips for ancient astronauts? We will delve into the various theories and examine the evidence that supports them. Additionally, we will uncover the secrets of the Incan Empire and the mysterious Lost City of Z, rumored to hold untold riches and ancient knowledge.

Unveiling Hidden Truths

As we journey through these ancient mysteries and lost civilizations, we will not only uncover hidden truths but also challenge the established narratives of history. Our exploration will reveal that the past is far more complex and mysterious than we have been led to believe. By examining the evidence and questioning the conventional wisdom, we will open our minds to the possibility that our understanding of history is incomplete, and that the true story of our past has yet to be fully revealed.

Prepare for the Journey

As we embark on this journey through time, I encourage you to approach these mysteries with an open mind and a spirit of curiosity. The truths we uncover may challenge your beliefs and shake the foundations of what you thought you knew about the world. But it is through this process of questioning and discovery that we can come closer to understanding the true nature of our existence and the hidden history of humanity.

Welcome to Part One of *Forbidden FREQUENCIES: Unveiling the World's Hidden Truths*. Let us begin our exploration into the ancient mysteries and lost civilizations that have shaped our world.

I

Chapter One: The Forgotten Empire of Atlantis

The legend of Atlantis has captivated human imagination for millennia. Described by the ancient Greek philosopher Plato in his dialogues "Timaeus" and "Critias," Atlantis was said to be an advanced and powerful civilization that existed approximately 9,000 years before Plato's time. According to the legend, Atlantis was a large island located beyond the "Pillars of Hercules" (the Strait of Gibraltar) and was a dominant naval power. However, in a single day and night of misfortune, Atlantis was swallowed by the sea and disappeared without a trace.

But was Atlantis merely a myth, or was there a real civilization behind the legend? In this chapter, we will explore the evidence and theories surrounding the existence of Atlantis, from ancient texts to modern scientific investigations. We will delve into the possible locations of Atlantis, its cultural and technological advancements, and the reasons for its sudden disappearance.

Plato's Account of Atlantis

Plato's description of Atlantis is the primary source of information about this mysterious civilization. According to Plato, Atlantis was a utopian society with a highly organized government, advanced technology, and a powerful military. The Atlanteans were wealthy and lived in luxurious cities with grand temples and impressive architecture. They possessed advanced knowledge of engineering, agriculture, and navigation, which allowed them to build impressive structures and dominate the seas.

The downfall of Atlantis, according to Plato, was due to the moral and spiritual decay of its inhabitants. As the Atlanteans became more corrupt and power-hungry, they provoked the wrath of the gods, leading to their ultimate destruction. The island was said to have sunk into the ocean in a cataclysmic event, erasing nearly all traces of its existence.

Possible Locations of Atlantis

Numerous theories have been proposed regarding the possible location of Atlantis. Some of the most compelling hypotheses include:

The Mediterranean Hypothesis

- Some researchers believe that Atlantis was located in the Mediterranean Sea, near the island of Crete or Santorini. The Minoan civilization, which flourished on Crete and was known for its advanced culture and technology, is often linked to Atlantis. The volcanic eruption on Santorini around 1600 BCE could have caused a massive tsunami, leading to the destruction of the Minoan civilization and inspiring the legend of Atlantis.

The Atlantic Ocean Hypothesis

- Another popular theory places Atlantis in the Atlantic Ocean, possibly near the Azores or the Canary Islands. Proponents of this theory argue that the geological features of these islands match Plato's description of Atlantis as a large island with surrounding smaller islands.

The Caribbean Hypothesis

- Some researchers suggest that Atlantis was located in the Caribbean, possibly near the Bahamas or Cuba. The submerged structures found off the coast of Bimini, known as the Bimini Road, have been cited as evidence of an ancient civilization that could be linked to Atlantis.

The Antarctica Hypothesis

- A more controversial theory proposes that Atlantis was located in Antarctica, which was once a temperate continent before it was covered in ice. This hypothesis suggests that a shift in the Earth's crust caused Antarctica to move to its current position, leading to the freezing and submersion of Atlantis.

Cultural and Technological Advancements

The descriptions of Atlantis provided by Plato suggest a civilization that was far more advanced than other contemporary societies. Some of the notable advancements attributed to the Atlanteans include:

Engineering and Architecture

- The Atlanteans were said to have built impressive structures, including grand temples, palaces, and an extensive canal system. They used advanced engineering techniques to construct these buildings, which were made from a combination of stone and precious metals.

Agriculture

- Atlantis was described as a fertile land with abundant resources. The Atlanteans practiced advanced agricultural techniques, including irrigation and crop rotation, which allowed them to sustain a large population.

Navigation and Maritime Power

- As a dominant naval power, the Atlanteans possessed advanced knowledge of navigation and shipbuilding. They were able to explore and colonize distant lands, establishing a vast maritime empire.

Theories on the Disappearance of Atlantis

The sudden disappearance of Atlantis has been the subject of much speculation and debate. Some of the most popular theories include:

Natural Disasters

- Many researchers believe that Atlantis was destroyed by a natural disaster, such as a massive volcanic eruption, earthquake, or tsunami. These events could have caused the island to sink into the ocean, erasing nearly all traces of its existence.

Extraterrestrial Intervention

- Some theories suggest that Atlantis was destroyed by extra-terrestrial beings or advanced technology. This hypothesis posits that the Atlanteans may have had contact with alien civilizations, which ultimately led to their downfall.

Crustal Displacement

- The theory of crustal displacement suggests that a shift in the Earth's crust caused Atlantis to move to a different location, leading to its submersion and eventual disappearance. This hypothesis is often linked to the Antarctica theory, which proposes that Atlantis was once located on the continent before it was covered in ice.

Modern Investigations and Discoveries

In recent years, there have been several modern investigations and discoveries that have reignited interest in the legend of Atlantis. Underwater archaeological expeditions have uncovered submerged structures and artifacts that some researchers believe could be linked to the lost civilization. Additionally, advances in technology, such as satellite imaging and sonar mapping, have provided new tools for exploring potential sites of Atlantis.

Conclusion

The legend of Atlantis continues to captivate and inspire, offering a tantalizing glimpse into a possible ancient civilization that was far more advanced than we can imagine. While definitive proof of Atlantis remains elusive, the ongoing search for its remnants pushes the boundaries of our understanding and challenges us to rethink the history of human civilization. As we continue to explore the mysteries of our past, we may one day uncover the truth behind the legend of Atlantis.

2

Chapter Two: The Mysteries of Egypt

Egypt, the land of the pharaohs, is a place where history and mythology intertwine. For centuries, scholars and adventurers have been drawn to its ancient monuments, seeking to unravel the secrets of one of the world's oldest and most enigmatic civilizations. The Great Pyramids of Giza, the Sphinx, and countless other relics stand as testaments to a culture that possessed knowledge and technology far beyond what we often attribute to ancient societies. In this chapter, we will delve into the mysteries of Egypt, exploring the construction of the pyramids, the secrets of the Sphinx, and the hidden texts that may hold the key to understanding this ancient civilization.

The Great Pyramids of Giza

The Great Pyramids of Giza are among the most iconic structures in the world. Built during the Fourth Dynasty of the Old Kingdom, these monumental tombs have captivated imaginations for millennia. The largest of them, the Great Pyramid of Khufu, was the tallest man-made structure in the world for over 3,800 years. Despite extensive study, many aspects of their construction remain a mystery.

Construction Techniques

- The precise methods used to build the pyramids have been the subject of debate for centuries. Traditional theories suggest that massive limestone and granite blocks were transported from quarries and lifted into place using ramps. However, the logistics of such an endeavor, involving tens of thousands of workers and millions of blocks, remain unclear. Some researchers propose alternative theories, including the use of advanced tools and techniques, possibly even knowledge lost to history.

Mathematical Precision

- The pyramids are aligned with astonishing precision to the cardinal points, and their dimensions reflect advanced mathematical knowledge. The ratio of the perimeter to the height of the Great Pyramid, for instance, approximates the value of 2π. This suggests that the ancient Egyptians had a sophisticated understanding of geometry and possibly even astronomy.

Purpose and Symbolism

- While the pyramids are traditionally understood as tombs for the pharaohs, some researchers believe they may have served additional purposes. Theories range from astronomical observatories to repositories of esoteric knowledge. The precise layout of the pyramids and their alignment with certain stars have led some to suggest that they were part of a grand design reflecting the Egyptians' cosmological beliefs.

The Sphinx

The Great Sphinx of Giza, with its lion's body and human head, stands as one of the most enigmatic monuments of ancient Egypt. Carved from a single limestone ridge, it is believed to represent the pharaoh Khafre. However, much about the Sphinx remains shrouded in mystery.

Age and Origin

- Traditional dating places the construction of the Sphinx around 2500 BCE, during the reign of Khafre. However, some researchers argue that the weathering patterns on the Sphinx suggest it is much older, possibly predating the pyramids themselves. This theory, known as the water erosion hypothesis, posits that the Sphinx may have been carved during a wetter period in Egypt's distant past, which would push its construction back several thousand years.

Purpose and Function

- The exact purpose of the Sphinx is still debated. It is commonly thought to be a guardian figure, protecting the Giza plateau. However, its alignment with the constellation Leo during the spring equinox around 10,500 BCE has led some to propose that it served as an astronomical marker or part of a larger complex related to ancient Egyptian cosmology.

Hidden Chambers

- Legends and modern research both suggest the possibility of hidden chambers beneath the Sphinx. Using ground-penetrating radar, scientists have identified anomalies that could indicate voids or tunnels. These hidden chambers, if they exist, may contain valuable artifacts or texts that could shed light on the Sphinx's true origins and purpose.

Hidden Texts and Esoteric Knowledge

Beyond the monumental architecture, Egypt is also home to a wealth of texts and inscriptions that provide insight into the culture's beliefs and knowledge. Some of these texts are well-known, while others remain hidden or misunderstood.

The Emerald Tablets

- Among the most famous of these esoteric texts are the Emerald Tablets of Thoth, said to contain the secrets of alchemy and the universe. These tablets, attributed to the mythical figure Hermes Trismegistus, are thought to hold profound wisdom about the nature of reality and the spiritual transformation of the soul.

The Book of the Dead

- The Egyptian Book of the Dead, a collection of spells and incantations intended to guide the deceased through the afterlife, offers a glimpse into the ancient Egyptians' beliefs about death and rebirth. This text, inscribed on papyrus and tomb walls, reflects a sophisticated understanding of the spiritual journey and the importance of maintaining balance and harmony.

The Edfu Texts

- Less well-known are the Edfu Texts, inscriptions found in the Temple of Edfu that describe the creation of the world and the founding of Egypt. These texts, which are often overlooked by mainstream scholars, contain references to a primordial time when gods walked the earth and established the first divine kingship. Some researchers believe these texts may preserve memories of a lost civilization predating dynastic Egypt.

Conclusion

The mysteries of Egypt continue to captivate and intrigue, offering tantalizing glimpses into a civilization that was both advanced and enigmatic. The Great Pyramids, the Sphinx, and the hidden texts all point to a culture that possessed profound knowledge and wisdom. As we continue to explore and study these ancient relics, we move closer to understanding the true nature of this remarkable civilization. The journey through Egypt's mysteries is far from over, and each new discovery brings us one step closer to uncovering the secrets of the past.

3

Chapter Three: The Mysteries of South American Civilizations

South America is a land rich in history, culture, and mystery. Long before the arrival of European explorers, advanced civilizations flourished across this vast continent, leaving behind monumental structures and enigmatic artifacts that continue to puzzle researchers and archaeologists. Among these mysteries are the Nazca Lines, the technological marvels of the Incan Empire, and the elusive Lost City of Z. In this chapter, we will explore these wonders, delving into the theories and evidence that surround these ancient South American civilizations.

The Nazca Lines

The Nazca Lines, a series of large geoglyphs etched into the desert plains of southern Peru, are among the most enigmatic creations of the ancient world. These lines, which form geometric shapes, animals, and humanoid figures, stretch across an area of nearly 1,000 square kilometers. Visible only from the air, the purpose and construction of the Nazca Lines have sparked countless theories and debates.

Creation and Construction

- The Nazca Lines were created by removing the reddish-brown iron oxide-coated pebbles that cover the desert surface, revealing the light-colored earth beneath. This simple yet effective technique allowed the Nazca people to create large and precise designs. The sheer scale and accuracy of these geoglyphs raise questions about the methods and tools used by the ancient Nazca culture.

Purpose and Theories

- The purpose of the Nazca Lines remains one of the greatest mysteries of the ancient world. Several theories have been proposed to explain their function:
  - **Astronomical Calendar:** Some researchers believe

the lines were used as an astronomical calendar, aligning with celestial bodies to mark important dates and events.

- **Religious or Ceremonial Sites:** Another theory suggests that the lines were part of religious or ceremonial practices, possibly related to water worship or fertility rituals.
- **Pathways and Pilgrimages:** Some scholars propose that the lines served as pathways for religious pilgrimages or processions.
- **Extraterrestrial Connections:** The most controversial theory posits that the Nazca Lines were created or influenced by extraterrestrial beings, serving as landing strips or messages to ancient astronauts.

The Incan Empire

The Incan Empire, known as Tawantinsuyu in the Quechua language, was the largest and most sophisticated civilization in pre-Columbian America. At its height, the empire stretched across modern-day Peru, Ecuador, Bolivia, Argentina, Chile, and Colombia. The Incas are renowned for their architectural prowess, agricultural innovations, and complex societal organization.

Architectural Marvels

- The Incas are perhaps best known for their architectural achievements. Using precisely cut stones that fit together without mortar, they constructed impressive structures that have withstood the test of time. Notable examples include:
  - **Machu Picchu:** The most famous Incan site, Machu Picchu is a marvel of engineering, perched high in the Andes Mountains. Its purpose remains debated,

with theories ranging from a royal estate to a religious sanctuary.

- **Sacsayhuamán:** Located near Cusco, this fortress features massive stone walls that demonstrate the Incas' mastery of stonework and engineering.
- **Ollantaytambo:** An archaeological site that includes a fortress, agricultural terraces, and a complex urban layout.

Agricultural Innovations

- The Incas developed advanced agricultural techniques to sustain their large population in the challenging Andean environment. They constructed terraces to prevent soil erosion and manage water resources effectively. Additionally, they created a network of storage facilities, known as colcas, to store surplus crops and ensure food security.

Societal Organization

- The Incan society was highly organized, with a centralized government led by the Sapa Inca. The empire was divided into administrative units, each overseen by officials who reported directly to the central authority. The Incas also developed an extensive road system, known as the Qhapaq Ñan, which facilitated communication, trade, and military movements across the vast empire.

The Lost City of Z

The Lost City of Z, also known as El Dorado, is a legendary city believed to be located deep within the Amazon rainforest. The city was said to be rich in gold and other treasures, attracting countless explorers and adventurers in search of its fabled wealth.

Percy Fawcett and the Quest for Z

- The most famous explorer associated with the search for the Lost City of Z is Percy Fawcett, a British archaeologist and adventurer. In the early 20th century, Fawcett embarked on several expeditions into the Amazon, convinced that an advanced civilization once thrived in the region. In 1925, Fawcett, along with his son and another companion, disappeared without a trace while searching for the city. Their fate remains unknown, adding to the legend and mystique of the Lost City of Z.

Modern Discoveries and Theories

- In recent years, advances in technology have led to new discoveries in the Amazon that suggest the existence of complex societies. Researchers using LiDAR (Light Detection and Ranging) technology have uncovered evidence of ancient cities, extensive road networks, and sophisticated agricultural systems hidden beneath the dense jungle canopy. These findings support the idea that the Amazon was once home to large, organized civilizations, lending credibility to the legends of the Lost City of Z.

Conclusion

The mysteries of South American civilizations continue to captivate and intrigue, offering tantalizing glimpses into the ingenuity and sophistication of ancient cultures. The Nazca Lines, the architectural and agricultural achievements of the Incas, and the elusive Lost City of Z all point to a rich and complex history that remains partially hidden. As we continue to explore and study these ancient wonders, we move closer to uncovering the secrets of South America's past. The journey through these mysteries is far from over, and each new discovery brings us one step closer to understanding the true nature of these remarkable civilizations.

INTRODUCTION TO PART TWO

Occult Practices and Esoteric Teachings

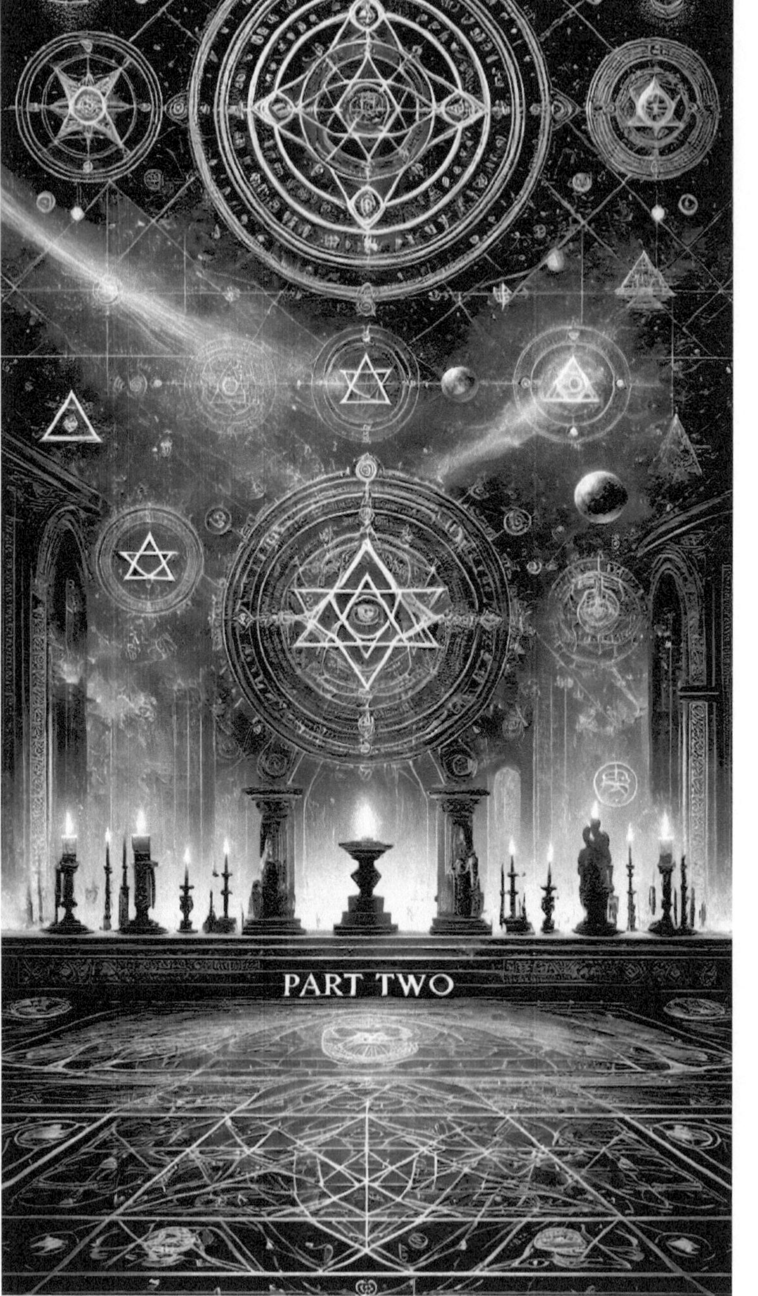
PART TWO

Throughout history, humanity has been fascinated by the unseen forces that shape our reality. From the ancient alchemists to modern mystics, individuals have sought to understand and harness these forces, often treading paths that diverge from mainstream religious and scientific thought. In Part Two of *Forbidden FREQUENCIES: Unveiling the World's Hidden Truths*, we delve into the world of occult practices and esoteric teachings, exploring the hidden wisdom that has been passed down through the ages.

The Allure of the Occult

The term "occult" comes from the Latin word "occultus," meaning hidden or secret. It refers to the study and practice of mystical, supernatural, or magical beliefs and phenomena that lie beyond the ordinary understanding of the world. The allure of the occult lies in its promise of hidden knowledge and power, offering insights into the mysteries of the universe and the potential to transcend ordinary human limitations.

Occult practices have taken many forms throughout history, from the ceremonial magic of the ancient Egyptians and Greeks to the alchemical traditions of medieval Europe and the modern-day practices of Wicca and Thelema. Despite their diversity, these practices share a common goal: to uncover the hidden truths of existence and attain a deeper understanding of the self and the cosmos.

Esoteric Teachings: The Inner Mysteries

Closely related to the occult are esoteric teachings, which refer to knowledge that is intended to be understood by a select group of individuals who have undergone a process of initiation or spiritual awakening. Esotericism encompasses a wide range of spiritual traditions and philosophies, including Gnosticism, Hermeticism, Kabbalah, and Rosicrucianism.

Esoteric teachings often emphasize the importance of personal transformation and the development of inner wisdom. They propose that true knowledge cannot be gained solely through external means, but must be experienced and internalized through spiritual practices and inner work. This journey inward is often depicted as a path of enlightenment, where the seeker transcends the illusions of the material world and attains a direct connection with the divine.

The Gnostic Quest for Knowledge

One of the most influential esoteric traditions is Gnosticism, which emerged in the early centuries of the Common Era. Gnostics believed that the material world was created by a lesser, malevolent deity and that true salvation lay in escaping this flawed creation and returning to the divine realm of pure spirit. Central to Gnostic belief was the concept of gnosis, or direct experiential knowledge of the divine.

Gnostic teachings were often suppressed by orthodox religious authorities, leading to the destruction of many Gnostic texts and the persecution of their followers. However, the discovery of the Nag Hammadi library in 1945, a collection of Gnostic texts buried in the Egyptian desert, has provided modern scholars with valuable insights into this enigmatic tradition.

The Alchemical Tradition

Alchemy, the precursor to modern chemistry, is another key aspect of esoteric teachings. Alchemists sought to transform base metals into gold and discover the elixir of life, a substance that would grant immortality. While these goals were often interpreted literally, alchemy also had a profound symbolic dimension, representing the spiritual transformation of the alchemist's soul.

The Hermetic tradition, which heavily influenced alchemy, attributed its teachings to Hermes Trismegistus, a mythical figure believed to be a fusion of the Greek god Hermes and the Egyptian god Thoth. Hermeticism emphasized the unity of all things and the correspondence between the macrocosm (the universe) and the microcosm (the individual). This principle, encapsulated in the phrase "As above, so below," is central to many esoteric and occult philosophies.

Modern Occult Movements

In the modern era, the occult has experienced a resurgence of interest, with new movements and practices emerging alongside the revival of ancient traditions. Figures like Aleister Crowley, founder of Thelema, and Gerald Gardner, the father of modern Wicca, have left a lasting impact on contemporary occultism. These movements often blend elements of older esoteric traditions with new interpretations and practices, reflecting the evolving nature of occult knowledge.

The Quest for Hidden Knowledge

At its core, the study of occult practices and esoteric teachings is a quest for hidden knowledge and spiritual enlightenment. It invites us to look beyond the surface of reality and explore the deeper, often hidden, dimensions of existence. As we journey through this part of *Forbidden FREQUENCIES*, we will encounter a wealth of mystical traditions, secret societies, and arcane practices, each offering unique insights into the nature of the universe and our place within it.

Prepare to venture into the shadows and uncover the secrets that have been guarded for centuries. Welcome to Part Two: Occult Practices and Esoteric Teachings.

4

Chapter Four: The Forbidden Teachings of the Gnostics

CHAPTER
FOUR
CHAPTER FOUR

Gnosticism is a mystical and esoteric belief system that emerged in the early centuries of the Common Era, deeply influencing the religious and philosophical landscape of the time. Its adherents, known as Gnostics, sought to attain gnosis—a direct, experiential knowledge of the divine. Gnosticism presented a worldview that diverged sharply from orthodox Christianity, proposing a dualistic cosmos in which the material world was seen as a flawed creation of a lesser deity. This chapter explores the forbidden teachings of the Gnostics, their sacred texts, and the impact of their beliefs on the broader spiritual traditions.

Origins and Core Beliefs

Historical Background

- Gnosticism is believed to have emerged in the first and second centuries CE, during a period of significant religious and philosophical ferment. It drew upon elements of Jewish, Christian, Greco-Roman, and Eastern religious traditions, synthesizing them into a unique and often controversial worldview.

The Dualistic Cosmos

- Central to Gnostic belief is the concept of dualism—the idea that the material world is fundamentally flawed and corrupt, created by a lesser deity known as the Demiurge. In contrast, the spiritual realm is the domain of the true, transcendent God, a being of pure light and goodness. Humanity, according to Gnostics, is trapped in the material world, but possesses a divine spark that can be liberated through gnosis.

The Divine Spark

- Gnostics believed that within each individual resides a fragment of the divine essence, a spark that has become entrapped in the material world. The goal of Gnostic practice is to awaken this divine spark and achieve spiritual liberation, returning to the true God.

Sacred Texts and Gospels

The Nag Hammadi Library

- One of the most significant discoveries shedding light on Gnostic teachings is the Nag Hammadi library, a collection of ancient texts unearthed in Egypt in 1945. These texts, written in Coptic, include a variety of Gnostic scriptures, gospels, and philosophical treatises. Among the most famous are the Gospel of Thomas, the Gospel of Philip, and the Gospel of Truth.

The Gospel of Thomas

- The Gospel of Thomas is a collection of sayings attributed to Jesus, many of which are strikingly different from those found in the canonical New Testament. It emphasizes direct, personal experience of the divine, encouraging readers to seek the light within themselves.

The Gospel of Philip

- The Gospel of Philip explores themes of sacramental mysticism and the nature of the divine. It contains enigmatic passages about the spiritual significance of marriage and the union of opposites, reflecting Gnostic beliefs about the restoration of spiritual wholeness.

The Gospel of Truth

- The Gospel of Truth presents a poetic and philosophical reflection on the nature of ignorance and enlightenment. It portrays the material world as a realm of illusion and error, from which souls must be awakened through knowledge of the true God.

The Archons: Manipulators of the Material World

Nature and Role of the Archons

- In Gnostic cosmology, the Archons are powerful, malevolent beings who serve the Demiurge. They are seen as rulers of the material world, responsible for maintaining the illusion and enslavement of souls. The Archons are often depicted as obstructing spiritual progress and trapping souls in the cycle of reincarnation.

Overcoming the Archons

- Gnostic teachings offer various methods for overcoming the influence of the Archons, including the practice of asceticism, meditation, and the use of esoteric knowledge and rituals. The ultimate goal is to transcend the material world and return to the divine source.

Modern Gnosticism and Its Revival

Contemporary Gnostic Movements

- Despite centuries of suppression, Gnostic ideas have experienced a revival in the modern era. Contemporary Gnostic movements, such as the Ecclesia Gnostica and the

Gnostic Society, seek to reclaim and reinterpret the ancient teachings for a modern audience. These groups often emphasize personal spiritual experience and the pursuit of inner knowledge.

Influence on Modern Spirituality

- Gnostic themes have also permeated broader spiritual and philosophical currents, influencing everything from New Age thought to depth psychology. The emphasis on personal gnosis, the critique of materialism, and the quest for spiritual awakening resonate with many contemporary seekers.

Conclusion

The forbidden teachings of the Gnostics offer a profound and often challenging perspective on the nature of reality and the human condition. By positing a dualistic cosmos and emphasizing the importance of direct, experiential knowledge of the divine, Gnosticism invites us to question the assumptions of both orthodox religion and materialist philosophy. As we explore these ancient teachings, we uncover a rich tradition of mystical insight that continues to inspire and provoke thought in the modern world.

5

Chapter Five: Alchemy and the Quest for Immortality

Alchemy, often regarded as the precursor to modern chemistry, is a complex and multifaceted tradition that combines elements of science, philosophy, and mysticism. For centuries, alchemists sought to transform base metals into gold and discover the elixir of life—a substance that would grant immortality. However, beyond these literal interpretations, alchemy also represents a profound symbolic and spiritual quest for self-transformation and enlightenment. In this chapter, we will explore the history of alchemy, its core principles and practices, and its enduring influence on both science and spirituality.

Origins and Historical Context

Ancient Roots

- The origins of alchemy can be traced back to ancient Egypt, where it was practiced as early as 3000 BCE. The Egyptians believed that the gods had bestowed upon them the secrets of transformation and transmutation. The Greek word "chemia," from which "alchemy" is derived, means "black land" and refers to the fertile soil of Egypt, symbolizing the transformative power of nature.

Hermetic Tradition

- Alchemy flourished in the Hellenistic period, influenced by the teachings attributed to Hermes Trismegistus—a syncretic figure combining the Greek god Hermes and the Egyptian god Thoth. The Hermetic tradition emphasized the unity of all things and the correspondence between the macrocosm (the universe) and the microcosm (the individual). Hermetic texts, such as the Emerald Tablet, became foundational to alchemical thought.

Medieval and Renaissance Alchemy

- During the Middle Ages and the Renaissance, alchemy spread throughout the Islamic world and Europe. Islamic scholars translated and expanded upon Greek and Egyptian alchemical texts, preserving and enhancing the tradition. In medieval Europe, alchemy became intertwined with Christian mysticism, and alchemists such as Paracelsus and Nicholas Flamel gained fame for their purported discoveries and insights.

Core Principles and Practices

The Philosopher's Stone

- The Philosopher's Stone, also known as the "elixir," is one of the central symbols of alchemy. It was believed to have the power to transform base metals into gold and grant immortality. The Philosopher's Stone represents the culmination of the alchemist's quest for perfection and enlightenment—a metaphor for the spiritual transformation of the self.

The Magnum Opus

- The Magnum Opus, or "Great Work," refers to the alchemical process of achieving the Philosopher's Stone. This process is often depicted as a series of stages, each symbolizing a different aspect of transformation. The stages typically include:
  - **Nigredo (Blackening):** The initial stage of dissolution and purification, symbolizing the death of the old self.
  - **Albedo (Whitening):** The stage of purification and enlightenment, representing the emergence of the true self.

- **Citrinitas (Yellowing):** The stage of spiritual awakening and illumination.
- **Rubedo (Reddening):** The final stage of perfection and completion, symbolizing the attainment of the Philosopher's Stone.

Transmutation and the Four Elements

- Alchemists believed that all matter was composed of four elements: earth, water, air, and fire. The process of transmutation involved manipulating these elements to achieve transformation. Alchemical symbols and diagrams often depict the interaction of these elements, illustrating the principles of transformation and balance.

Symbolism and Spiritual Alchemy

Alchemy as a Metaphor for Inner Transformation

- While alchemy is often associated with the literal transformation of metals, many alchemists viewed their work as a metaphor for spiritual and psychological transformation. The process of turning lead into gold symbolized the purification and perfection of the soul. The alchemist's laboratory was seen as a sacred space where inner and outer transformations mirrored one another.

Alchemical Imagery and Symbols

- Alchemical texts and illustrations are rich with symbolic imagery, often depicting mythical creatures, celestial bodies, and complex geometric patterns. These symbols convey multiple layers of meaning, inviting the reader to contemplate the deeper truths they represent. Common alchemical symbols include the serpent (representing rebirth and renewal), the ouroboros (the serpent eating its own tail, symbolizing the cyclical nature of existence), and the phoenix (representing resurrection and immortality).

Alchemy's Influence on Science and Mysticism

Transition to Modern Chemistry

- Alchemy laid the groundwork for the development of modern chemistry. Alchemists' experiments with substances and their properties contributed to the understanding of chemical reactions and processes. The transition from alchemy to chemistry is marked by figures such as Robert Boyle and Antoine Lavoisier, who adopted empirical methods and rejected mystical interpretations.

Enduring Mystical and Philosophical Legacy

- Despite its transformation into modern science, alchemy's mystical and philosophical legacy endures. The principles of alchemy continue to influence various spiritual and esoteric traditions, including Jungian psychology. Carl Jung, a Swiss psychiatrist, and psychoanalyst, drew parallels between alchemical symbolism and the process of individuation—the journey toward self-realization and wholeness.

Conclusion

Alchemy represents a rich tapestry of science, mysticism, and philosophy, embodying humanity's quest for transformation and enlightenment. The pursuit of the Philosopher's Stone, whether as a literal substance or a metaphor for spiritual perfection, reflects the timeless desire to transcend the limitations of the material world and achieve a higher state of being. As we explore the alchemical tradition, we uncover a wealth of wisdom and insight that continues to inspire and challenge us on our own journeys of self-discovery.

6

Chapter Six: The Dark Arts and Black Magic

Throughout history, the allure of the dark arts and black magic has captivated and terrified people in equal measure. These practices, shrouded in mystery and often condemned by mainstream society, involve the invocation of supernatural forces for personal gain, power, or vengeance. In this chapter, we will explore the historical context of the dark arts, delve into the practices and rituals of black magic, and examine the ethical boundaries and moral implications of these forbidden paths.

Historical Context

Ancient Roots

- The origins of the dark arts can be traced back to ancient civilizations, where magic and religion were often intertwined. In ancient Egypt, for example, priests and magicians practiced complex rituals to invoke the gods and manipulate supernatural forces. Similarly, in Mesopotamia, sorcerers and shamans were believed to possess the power to control spirits and cast spells.

Medieval Witchcraft and the Inquisition

- During the Middle Ages, fear of witchcraft and black magic reached a fever pitch in Europe. The Catholic Church, viewing these practices as heretical and a threat to its authority, launched the Inquisition to root out and punish those accused of witchcraft. Thousands of people, mostly women, were tried, tortured, and executed in what became known as the witch hunts. These dark chapters in history reflect the pervasive fear and misunderstanding surrounding the practice of black magic.

Renaissance and Enlightenment

- The Renaissance saw a renewed interest in occult knowledge, with scholars and magicians like John Dee and Giordano Bruno exploring the boundaries of magic and science. While some sought to uncover the secrets of the universe through alchemy and astrology, others delved into darker realms, seeking to harness demonic powers and forbidden knowledge.

Practices and Rituals of Black Magic

The Grimoire Tradition

- Grimoires are ancient texts that serve as manuals for performing magical rituals and summoning supernatural entities. These books contain detailed instructions on how to cast spells, create talismans, and invoke spirits. Some of the most famous grimoires include the "Key of Solomon," the "Book of Abramelin," and the "Grand Grimoire." These texts often emphasize the importance of precise rituals, incantations, and the use of specific ingredients.

Summoning and Binding Spirits

- One of the core practices of black magic involves summoning and binding spirits or demons to do the practitioner's bidding. This process typically requires elaborate rituals, including the drawing of protective circles, the recitation of powerful incantations, and the use of magical symbols. The summoned entity is often bound to a physical object, such as a talisman or a mirror, and compelled to obey the magician's commands.

Curses and Hexes

- Black magic is often associated with the casting of curses and hexes to harm or manipulate others. These rituals aim to inflict physical, emotional, or spiritual suffering on the target. Common methods include creating poppets (voodoo dolls), using personal belongings or bodily fluids of the victim, and performing ritualistic actions intended to channel negative energy.

Necromancy

- Necromancy, the practice of communicating with the dead, is another aspect of black magic. Necromancers seek to summon and control the spirits of the deceased to gain knowledge, predict the future, or manipulate events in the living world. This practice often involves the use of grave-yard soil, bones, and other macabre elements in rituals designed to pierce the veil between life and death.

Ethical Boundaries and Moral Implications

The Ethics of Power and Control

- The pursuit of power and control through black magic raises significant ethical questions. Manipulating super-natural forces and other people for personal gain often involves violating the free will and autonomy of others. This exploitation of power can lead to destructive and harmful consequences, both for the practitioner and those affected by their actions.

The Consequences of Dark Magic

- Many traditions and belief systems warn of the potential dangers and repercussions of practicing black magic. These include physical and mental harm, spiritual corruption, and the possibility of invoking malevolent entities that can become difficult to control. The concept of karma, or the idea that one's actions have consequences that eventually return to the doer, is often cited as a reason to avoid the dark arts.

The Line Between Good and Evil

- The practice of black magic challenges the conventional notions of good and evil. While some practitioners justify their actions as necessary for self-defense or justice, others embrace the pursuit of power without regard for moral consequences. This ambiguity highlights the complex and often subjective nature of ethical boundaries in the realm of the supernatural.

Modern Practitioners and Black Magic Today

Contemporary Occultists

- In the modern era, the practice of black magic continues to thrive among certain occult communities. Contemporary practitioners often draw upon traditional grimoires and rituals, while also incorporating new elements and personal innovations. The internet has facilitated the spread of occult knowledge, allowing practitioners to connect, share, and refine their practices.

Pop Culture and Black Magic

- Black magic has also found a place in popular culture, often depicted in books, movies, and television shows. These portrayals range from sensationalized horror stories to more nuanced explorations of the ethical dilemmas faced by practitioners. While these fictional representations can perpetuate stereotypes and misconceptions, they also reflect the enduring fascination with the dark arts.

Conclusion

The dark arts and black magic represent a forbidden and often misunderstood aspect of human spirituality and the quest for power. From ancient rituals to modern practices, these traditions have captivated and terrified people across cultures and eras. By exploring the historical context, practices, and ethical implications of black magic, we gain a deeper understanding of the complex and multifaceted nature of the supernatural. As we continue to navigate the boundaries of the known and the unknown, the allure of the dark arts serves as a reminder of the power and peril that lie within the shadows.

INTRODUCTION TO PART THREE

Secret Societies and Hidden Agendas

PART THREE

Throughout history, secret societies have intrigued and captivated the imaginations of many. These enigmatic groups, often operating in the shadows, have been accused of manipulating events from behind the scenes, wielding power and influence far beyond their visible presence. Part Three of *Forbidden FREQUENCIES: Unveiling the World's Hidden Truths* delves into the mysterious world of secret societies and hidden agendas, exploring the historical roots, core beliefs, and alleged activities of some of the most notorious and influential groups in history.

The Allure of Secrecy

The very nature of secret societies—cloaked in mystery, guarded by oaths of secrecy, and often accessible only to a select few—makes them fertile ground for speculation and conspiracy theories. The allure of these groups lies in their promise of hidden knowledge, exclusive power, and the ability to influence world events. From the Freemasons and the Illuminati to the Bilderberg Group and beyond, secret societies have been both revered and feared, their true purposes and actions shrouded in ambiguity.

Historical Roots and Evolution

Ancient and Medieval Origins

- The origins of secret societies can be traced back to ancient civilizations. In ancient Egypt, the priesthoods of Isis and Osiris conducted esoteric rituals reserved for the initiated. In Greece, the Eleusinian Mysteries offered initiates profound spiritual insights through secret rites. During the Middle Ages, the Knights Templar emerged as a powerful and wealthy order, accused of heresy and ultimately disbanded, their wealth and secrets lost to history.

Renaissance and Enlightenment

○ The Renaissance saw the rise of new secret societies, blending ancient wisdom with emerging scientific knowledge. The Rosicrucians, a mystical and philosophical society, claimed to possess secret knowledge that could transform society. The Enlightenment further fueled the growth of secret societies, as intellectuals sought to challenge the established order and promote new ideas through clandestine networks.

Core Beliefs and Practices

Initiation and Ritual

○ Central to many secret societies is the practice of initiation, a formal process by which new members are introduced to the group's secrets and rituals. Initiation rites often involve symbolic death and rebirth, reflecting the transformative journey of the initiate. These rituals are designed to foster a deep sense of belonging and commitment to the society's ideals.

Esoteric Knowledge

○ Secret societies often claim to possess esoteric knowledge —hidden truths about the nature of reality, the universe, and humanity. This knowledge is typically revealed progressively, with higher levels of initiation granting access to deeper and more profound insights. The pursuit of this knowledge is seen as a path to personal and spiritual enlightenment.

Symbols and Allegory

○ Symbols play a crucial role in the teachings and rituals of secret societies. These symbols, often drawn from ancient mythologies and sacred geometries, serve as visual representations of complex philosophical concepts. Members are trained to interpret these symbols, unlocking layers of meaning and insight.

Notable Secret Societies

The Freemasons

- One of the most well-known secret societies, the Freemasons trace their origins to the medieval stonemason guilds. Freemasonry emphasizes moral development, brotherhood, and the pursuit of truth. Its elaborate rituals, hierarchical structure, and use of symbolic tools (such as the compass and square) have made it a subject of fascination and speculation.

The Illuminati

- Founded in 1776 by Adam Weishaupt, the Bavarian Illuminati sought to promote Enlightenment ideals and challenge the power of the church and monarchy. Despite being disbanded in the late 18th century, the Illuminati have persisted in popular imagination as the archetype of a secret society bent on world domination. Conspiracy theories about the Illuminati's influence on global events continue to abound.

The Bilderberg Group

- Established in 1954, the Bilderberg Group consists of influential political leaders, business executives, and intellectuals who meet annually to discuss global issues. The secretive nature of their meetings has led to widespread speculation about their true agenda, with some believing that the group orchestrates major geopolitical and economic decisions behind closed doors.

Hidden Agendas and Conspiracy Theories

Manipulation of World Events

- Secret societies are often accused of manipulating world events to serve their hidden agendas. From orchestrating wars and revolutions to controlling financial markets and political institutions, these groups are believed to wield disproportionate influence over global affairs. While concrete evidence is often lacking, the persistence of these theories reflects deep-seated anxieties about unseen powers shaping the course of history.

Control and Surveillance

- Another common theme in conspiracy theories about secret societies is the notion of surveillance and control. Groups like the Illuminati and the Freemasons are thought to employ sophisticated methods to monitor and influence individuals, maintaining their grip on power through covert means. The rise of digital surveillance technologies has only fueled these fears, blurring the line between fiction and reality.

Conclusion

The world of secret societies and hidden agendas is a labyrinthine realm where fact and fiction intertwine. These groups, with their mysterious rituals, esoteric knowledge, and alleged influence, challenge our understanding of power and control in the modern world. As we delve into the stories and theories surrounding these enigmatic organizations, we uncover a tapestry of intrigue and speculation that continues to captivate and provoke thought. Welcome to Part Three: Secret Societies and Hidden Agendas.

7

Chapter Seven: The Freemasons and Their Hidden Hand

The Freemasons are perhaps the most well-known and widely discussed secret society in history. With roots stretching back to the stonemason guilds of medieval Europe, the Freemasons have grown into a global fraternity with millions of members. Known for their intricate rituals, symbolic language, and secretive nature, the Freemasons have long been the subject of fascination and conspiracy theories. This chapter explores the origins, beliefs, and influence of the Freemasons, as well as the various myths and controversies that surround them.

Historical Origins

Medieval Stonemasons

- The origins of Freemasonry can be traced to the stonemason guilds of medieval Europe. These guilds were associations of craftsmen who built the cathedrals, castles, and other monumental structures of the time. They possessed specialized knowledge of geometry, engineering, and architecture, which they guarded closely. The guilds also had a system of degrees, or levels of mastery, through which members advanced based on their skill and experience.

Transition to Speculative Masonry

- In the late 16th and early 17th centuries, Freemasonry began to transition from an operative craft guild to a speculative fraternity. This shift involved the admission of "gentlemen Masons"—men who were not stonemasons by trade but were interested in the philosophical and symbolic aspects of the craft. These speculative Masons retained the guild's rituals and symbols, using them as allegories for moral and spiritual development.

The Founding of the Grand Lodge

○ The formal organization of Freemasonry began with the founding of the Grand Lodge of England in 1717. This event marked the establishment of a centralized authority for the fraternity and set the stage for the spread of Freemasonry throughout Europe and the Americas. The Grand Lodge system provided a framework for the creation of additional lodges, each governed by its own set of rules and traditions.

Core Beliefs and Practices

The Great Architect of the Universe

○ Freemasonry is founded on the belief in a Supreme Being, referred to as the Great Architect of the Universe. This concept emphasizes the importance of a guiding intelligence behind the creation and order of the cosmos. Freemasonry is non-denominational, allowing members to interpret the Great Architect in accordance with their own religious or spiritual beliefs.

Masonic Degrees and Rituals

○ Freemasonry is organized into a system of degrees, each representing a different level of knowledge and initiation. The three basic degrees are:
  - **Entered Apprentice:** The first degree, focusing on the candidate's introduction to the fraternity and the importance of self-improvement.
  - **Fellowcraft:** The second degree, emphasizing the development of intellectual and moral virtues.
  - **Master Mason:** The third degree, representing the culmination of the candidate's journey and the attainment of deeper esoteric knowledge.

- Each degree involves a series of rituals, including symbolic gestures, passwords, and oaths. These rituals are designed to convey moral lessons and reinforce the bonds of brotherhood among members.

Symbols and Allegory

- Freemasonry is rich with symbols and allegorical teachings. Some of the most prominent Masonic symbols include:
    - **The Square and Compasses:** Representing morality and the pursuit of truth.
    - **The Letter "G":** Often interpreted as standing for "God" or "Geometry," symbolizing the divine order of the universe.
    - **The All-Seeing Eye:** A symbol of divine watchfulness and the pursuit of enlightenment.
- These symbols are used to teach moral and philosophical principles, encouraging members to reflect on their personal growth and contributions to society.

Influence and Controversies

Freemasonry and the Enlightenment

- Freemasonry played a significant role in the intellectual and cultural movements of the Enlightenment. Many prominent thinkers, scientists, and political leaders of the 18th century were Freemasons, including Benjamin Franklin, Voltaire, and Wolfgang Amadeus Mozart. The fraternity's emphasis on reason, tolerance, and individual liberty resonated with the ideals of the Enlightenment, contributing to its widespread influence.

Political and Social Impact

- Throughout history, Freemasonry has been linked to various political and social movements. In the United States, Freemasons were instrumental in the founding of the nation, with many of the Founding Fathers, including George Washington and Thomas Jefferson, being members. Freemasonry's values of equality and fraternity also aligned with the principles of the French Revolution, leading to its involvement in revolutionary activities.

Myths and Conspiracy Theories

- The secretive nature of Freemasonry has given rise to numerous myths and conspiracy theories. Some of the most persistent allegations include:
    - **World Domination:** Conspiracy theorists claim that Freemasons seek to establish a New World Order, using their influence to control governments and economies.
    - **Occult Practices:** Freemasonry's use of symbols and rituals has led to accusations of occultism and devil worship. These claims are often based on misunderstandings or deliberate misrepresentations of Masonic teachings.
    - **Hidden Agendas:** Critics argue that Freemasonry operates as a shadowy cabal, advancing its own interests at the expense of the public good.
- Despite these controversies, Freemasonry continues to be a respected and influential organization, with millions of members worldwide.

Modern Freemasonry

Global Presence

○ Today, Freemasonry is a global fraternity, with lodges in nearly every country. While each lodge operates independently, they are united by common principles and traditions. Freemasonry's commitment to charity, education, and community service continues to be a central aspect of its mission.

Challenges and Adaptations

○ In recent years, Freemasonry has faced challenges, including declining membership and changing societal attitudes. To address these issues, some lodges have adopted new approaches to recruitment and outreach, emphasizing the relevance of Masonic values in the modern world.

Freemasonry in the Digital Age

○ The digital age has brought new opportunities and challenges for Freemasonry. Online forums, virtual lodges, and social media have allowed Masons to connect and share ideas across distances. However, the fraternity must also navigate the complexities of maintaining secrecy and tradition in an increasingly interconnected world.

Conclusion

The Freemasons represent a fascinating blend of tradition, philosophy, and mystery. From their medieval origins to their modern global presence, Freemasonry has played a significant role in shaping intellectual, cultural, and political landscapes. While surrounded by myths and controversies, the fraternity's core principles of brotherhood, moral development, and the pursuit of truth continue to inspire and guide its members. As we explore the hidden hand of the Freemasons, we gain a deeper understanding of their enduring influence and the values that underpin their secretive world.

8

Chapter Eight: The Illuminati and the Quest for Global Control

The Illuminati, a name that has become synonymous with conspiracy theories and secret plots for global domination, remains one of the most controversial and enigmatic secret societies in history. Founded in the late 18th century, the Illuminati has been linked to various political, economic, and social upheavals, often portrayed as a shadowy cabal wielding immense influence behind the scenes. This chapter delves into the origins, beliefs, and alleged activities of the Illuminati, examining the facts and fictions that have fueled its enduring mystique.

Origins and Historical Background

The Bavarian Illuminati

- The Illuminati was founded on May 1, 1776, by Adam Weishaupt, a professor of canon law at the University of Ingolstadt in Bavaria (modern-day Germany). Weishaupt sought to create an organization that would promote Enlightenment ideals such as reason, secularism, and the separation of church and state. The Illuminati aimed to combat religious and political oppression and to foster a society based on merit, knowledge, and the pursuit of truth.

Structure and Membership

- The Illuminati adopted a hierarchical structure, similar to that of the Freemasons, with multiple degrees of initiation. Members were drawn from various social strata, including intellectuals, politicians, and influential figures. The society operated under strict secrecy, using pseudonyms and coded communications to protect the identities of its members and its activities.

Suppression and Disbandment

- The Illuminati's anti-clerical and anti-monarchical stance quickly drew the ire of the Bavarian authorities. In 1784, Duke Karl Theodor of Bavaria issued an edict banning all secret societies, including the Illuminati. Weishaupt was forced into exile, and many members were arrested or went underground. By the late 1780s, the Illuminati had largely disbanded, but its legacy continued to inspire fear and speculation.

Beliefs and Ideals

Enlightenment Principles

- At its core, the Illuminati embraced the principles of the Enlightenment. Members sought to promote rational thought, scientific inquiry, and the separation of religious and political institutions. They believed in the power of education and knowledge to transform society and liberate individuals from ignorance and tyranny.

Human Perfectibility

- The Illuminati espoused the belief in the perfectibility of humanity. They held that through education, moral development, and social reform, individuals and society as a whole could achieve a state of enlightenment and progress. This optimistic vision stood in stark contrast to the conservative and religious institutions of the time.

Secret Influence

- The Illuminati believed in the necessity of operating behind the scenes to effect change. Given the repressive political climate of the 18th century, they saw secrecy as essential to their mission. This clandestine approach has fueled countless conspiracy theories, suggesting that the Illuminati continues to wield covert power.

Conspiracy Theories and Modern Allegations

The French Revolution

- One of the earliest conspiracy theories involving the Illuminati posits that they orchestrated the French Revolution. Critics claimed that Illuminati agents infiltrated revolutionary groups, using their influence to topple the monarchy and establish a secular republic. While there is no concrete evidence to support this theory, it highlights the fear and suspicion that the Illuminati aroused.

New World Order

- Perhaps the most persistent and pervasive conspiracy theory is the idea that the Illuminati seeks to establish a New World Order—a totalitarian global government controlled by a select elite. Proponents of this theory argue that the Illuminati manipulates world events, from economic crises to wars, to advance their agenda of global domination. Symbols such as the pyramid and the all-seeing eye on the US dollar bill are often cited as evidence of their influence.

Cultural Influence

- The Illuminati has also been linked to various cultural and entertainment phenomena. Some conspiracy theorists claim that prominent musicians, actors, and public figures are members of the Illuminati, using their platforms to spread subliminal messages and maintain control over the masses. The prevalence of Illuminati symbols in music videos, movies, and fashion is cited as proof of their reach.

The Real Illuminati Today

Continued Influence or Myth?

- Despite the lack of concrete evidence, belief in the Illuminati's existence and influence persists. Some argue that the Illuminati continues to operate in secrecy, adapting to modern contexts and maintaining their agenda through hidden networks. Others contend that the Illuminati is a myth, a convenient scapegoat for explaining complex social and political phenomena.

Academic Perspectives

- Historians and scholars generally view the Illuminati as a product of its time—a radical intellectual movement that was quickly suppressed. They argue that the society's influence was limited and that the modern image of the Illuminati as an omnipotent conspiracy is largely a fabrication of popular culture and paranoia.

Conclusion

The Illuminati remains one of the most enigmatic and controversial secret societies in history. From its Enlightenment roots to its association with modern conspiracy theories, the Illuminati embodies the tension between knowledge and power, secrecy and transparency. Whether as a historical reality or a symbol of hidden influence, the Illuminati continues to captivate the imagination, challenging us to question the forces that shape our world. As we conclude this exploration, we are reminded of the enduring allure of the unknown and the power of ideas to transcend time and context.

9

Chapter Nine: The Bilderberg Group and the Elites Behind Closed Doors

CHAPTER NINE

The Bilderberg Group is one of the most secretive and controversial gatherings of influential leaders in the world. Founded in the mid-20th century, the group brings together political leaders, business magnates, and intellectuals for annual meetings held in complete secrecy. Critics argue that the Bilderberg Group wields significant power over global affairs, shaping policies and decisions that affect millions of people without any public scrutiny. This chapter delves into the origins, membership, and influence of the Bilderberg Group, as well as the conspiracy theories and controversies that surround it.

Origins and Historical Background

The Birth of Bilderberg

- The Bilderberg Group was founded in 1954 by Prince Bernhard of the Netherlands. The first meeting was held at the Hotel de Bilderberg in Oosterbeek, Netherlands, giving the group its name. The primary goal was to foster dialogue between Europe and North America during the Cold War, promoting cooperation and understanding to prevent another global conflict.

Early Meetings and Objectives

- The early meetings of the Bilderberg Group focused on strengthening the transatlantic alliance and addressing economic and political issues of mutual concern. Participants included politicians, business leaders, and academics, who engaged in off-the-record discussions designed to foster mutual understanding and collaboration.

Membership and Structure

Exclusive Invitations

◦ Membership in the Bilderberg Group is by invitation only, and attendees are selected for their influence and expertise. The group typically includes around 120-150 participants, with a mix of regular attendees and new invitees each year. The meetings are held under the Chatham House Rule, which allows participants to use the information shared but prohibits them from revealing the identities of the speakers or other participants.

Influential Participants

◦ Over the years, the Bilderberg Group has included some of the most powerful and influential figures in the world. Past attendees have included U.S. Presidents, European Prime Ministers, CEOs of major corporations, and leading intellectuals. The list of participants is often kept secret, fueling speculation about the group's true purpose and influence.

The Bilderberg Agenda

Topics of Discussion

◦ The topics discussed at Bilderberg meetings cover a wide range of issues, including global security, economic policy, technological innovation, and geopolitical developments. The agenda is set by the group's Steering Committee, which selects the themes and speakers for each meeting. The discussions are intended to be candid and informal, allowing participants to explore complex issues without the constraints of official positions or media scrutiny.

Influence and Impact

- Critics argue that the Bilderberg Group wields significant influence over global affairs, shaping policies and decisions that affect millions of people. While the group does not have formal decision-making power, the informal nature of the meetings allows participants to network and build consensus on important issues. Supporters of the group argue that these discussions help promote understanding and cooperation among global leaders.

Controversies and Conspiracy Theories

Secrecy and Lack of Transparency

- The secretive nature of the Bilderberg meetings has led to widespread suspicion and criticism. Critics argue that the lack of transparency undermines democratic principles and allows a small elite to wield disproportionate influence over global affairs. The group's insistence on secrecy has fueled numerous conspiracy theories, with some alleging that the Bilderberg Group is part of a broader effort to establish a New World Order.

New World Order Theories

- One of the most persistent conspiracy theories about the Bilderberg Group is that it seeks to establish a New World Order—a centralized global government controlled by a select elite. Proponents of this theory argue that the group's discussions and decisions are aimed at consolidating power and undermining national sovereignty. While there is no concrete evidence to support these claims, the theory remains popular among conspiracy theorists.

Corporate Influence

○ Another common criticism of the Bilderberg Group is the presence of corporate leaders and the potential for undue influence by big business. Critics argue that the group's discussions often prioritize the interests of multinational corporations over those of ordinary citizens. The close ties between political leaders and corporate executives at Bilderberg meetings have raised concerns about conflicts of interest and the erosion of democratic accountability.

The Reality of Bilderberg

A Forum for Dialogue

○ Despite the controversies and conspiracy theories, many participants and observers argue that the Bilderberg Group is simply a forum for dialogue and discussion. The off-the-record nature of the meetings allows participants to speak candidly and explore new ideas without fear of public backlash. While the group does bring together influential figures, its impact on global affairs is often overstated.

The Role of Think Tanks and Policy Institutes

○ The Bilderberg Group is part of a broader ecosystem of think tanks, policy institutes, and international organizations that facilitate dialogue among global leaders. Groups like the Council on Foreign Relations, the Trilateral Commission, and the World Economic Forum play similar roles in bringing together influential figures to discuss important issues. While these organizations can shape public policy, they do not operate as shadow governments.

Conclusion

The Bilderberg Group remains one of the most secretive and controversial gatherings of global leaders. While its meetings provide a valuable forum for dialogue and discussion, the lack of transparency and the presence of powerful figures have fueled numerous conspiracy theories and criticisms. Understanding the reality of the Bilderberg Group requires a nuanced perspective, recognizing both its role in fostering international cooperation and the legitimate concerns about its influence and secrecy. As we continue to explore the hidden worlds of secret societies and elite gatherings, the Bilderberg Group serves as a reminder of the complex interplay between power, secrecy, and public accountability.

INTRODUCTION TO PART FOUR

Government Cover-Ups and Modern Conspiracies

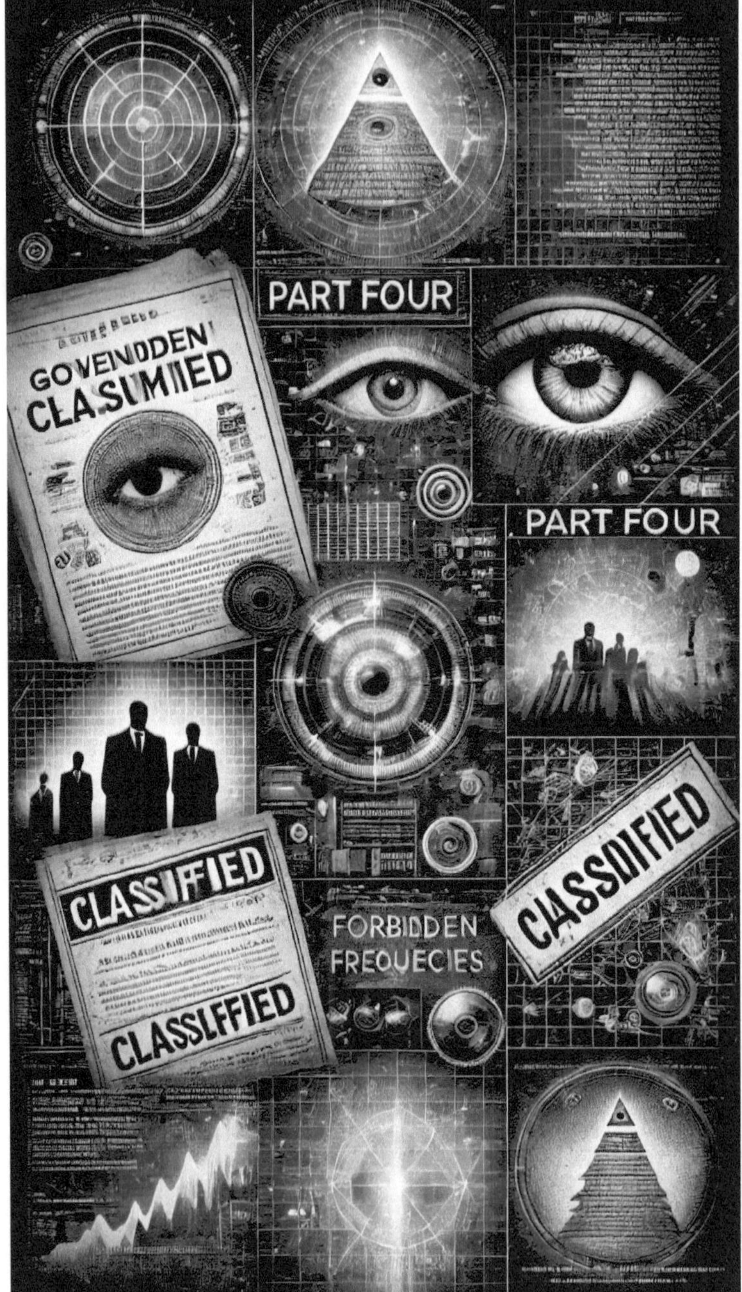
PART FOUR
PART FOUR
GOVENDDEN CLASUMIED
CLASSIFIED
CLASSLFFIED
CLASSIDIFIED
FORBIDDEN FREQUECIES

In the shadowy realms of power and influence, there exists a persistent belief that not everything is as it seems. From clandestine operations to outright deception, the idea that governments engage in cover-ups and conspiracies has captivated the public imagination for decades. Part Four of *Forbidden FREQUENCIES: Unveiling the World's Hidden Truths* delves into the murky waters of governmental secrecy, exploring the theories and evidence that suggest a hidden hand orchestrating events behind the scenes.

The Nature of Government Cover-Ups

Governments, by their very nature, wield enormous power and control. They have the capability to shape economies, influence societal norms, and direct the course of nations. With such power comes the temptation—and sometimes the perceived necessity—to hide certain truths from the public. Whether for national security, political advantage, or social stability, the reasons for government cover-ups are as varied as they are controversial.

Historical Precedents

Throughout history, there have been numerous instances where governments have been caught in acts of deception or secrecy. These historical precedents fuel contemporary conspiracy theories and provide a foundation for understanding how and why governments might engage in such behavior.

Operation Northwoods

- One of the most notorious examples of a proposed government conspiracy is Operation Northwoods, a plan developed by the U.S. Department of Defense in 1962. The plan suggested that the U.S. government could stage false-flag terrorist attacks against its own citizens to justify a war against Cuba. Although the plan was never implemented, its mere existence has been used to argue that governments are capable of extreme measures to achieve their objectives.

MKUltra

- Project MKUltra, conducted by the CIA from the 1950s to the 1970s, involved experiments on human subjects to develop mind control techniques. The project included the use of drugs, hypnosis, and other forms of psychological manipulation. The details of MKUltra were kept secret for decades, and its revelation has led to ongoing debates about the ethical boundaries of government experimentation.

Modern Conspiracies

In the contemporary world, new conspiracy theories continue to emerge, fueled by the internet and a growing distrust of authority. These theories often build on historical precedents and are amplified by the rapid dissemination of information and misinformation online.

The Surveillance State

- The revelations by whistleblowers like Edward Snowden have brought to light the extent of government surveillance on citizens. The notion of a surveillance state, where governments monitor and record the activities of their populations, has sparked widespread concern and debate about privacy and civil liberties.

False Flag Operations

- The idea that governments stage attacks or incidents to

manipulate public opinion and justify actions is a recurring theme in conspiracy theories. Events like the September 11 attacks have been scrutinized by theorists who believe that the official explanations do not account for all the evidence, suggesting instead that these incidents were orchestrated or allowed to happen to further specific agendas.

Secret Societies and Shadow Governments

- The belief in shadow governments or secret societies like the Illuminati or the Bilderberg Group controlling world events from behind the scenes is a persistent element of modern conspiracy theories. These theories suggest that real power is held by a small, unelected elite who operate beyond public scrutiny.

The Psychology of Conspiracy Theories

Understanding why people believe in conspiracy theories is crucial to grasping their impact on society. Several psychological factors contribute to the appeal of these theories:

Pattern Recognition

- Humans have a natural tendency to seek patterns and make sense of complex information. Conspiracy theories often provide a coherent narrative that explains chaotic or frightening events, offering a sense of control and understanding.

Distrust of Authority

- Historical instances of governmental deception and

corruption have fostered a deep-seated distrust of authority. This skepticism makes people more susceptible to believing that governments are capable of more sinister actions than they admit.

Social Identity

- Conspiracy theories can strengthen group identity, providing a sense of belonging to those who see themselves as part of a knowledgeable minority who understand the "truth" behind events.

The Impact on Society

The prevalence of conspiracy theories has significant implications for society. While some theories may uncover genuine abuses of power, many others can lead to harmful consequences, such as eroding trust in institutions, spreading misinformation, and inciting violence.

Conclusion

The exploration of government cover-ups and modern conspiracies reveals a complex interplay between truth, deception, and belief. As we delve into these controversial topics in Part Four of *Forbidden FREQUENCIES*, we are challenged to question our assumptions, critically evaluate evidence, and remain vigilant about the power dynamics that shape our world. The journey through these hidden realms invites us to uncover the truths that lie beneath the surface and to understand the forces that drive both secrecy and revelation.

10

Chapter Ten: Area 51 and the Extraterrestrial Cover-Up

AREA 51
AREA 51
CHAPTER TEN

Area 51, a highly secretive military base located in the Nevada desert, has become synonymous with conspiracy theories about extraterrestrial life and government cover-ups. For decades, this remote installation has been the focal point of speculation and intrigue, fueled by its mysterious activities and the government's tight-lipped stance. This chapter delves into the history, alleged secrets, and ongoing mysteries surrounding Area 51, exploring the claims of extraterrestrial encounters and the government's role in concealing the truth.

Historical Background

Origins and Development

- Area 51, officially known as Groom Lake or Homey Airport, was established in the early 1950s as a testing site for the U-2 spy plane. Its remote location and restricted airspace made it an ideal spot for testing top-secret aircraft away from prying eyes. Over the years, the base has been used to develop and test various advanced military technologies, including the SR-71 Blackbird and the F-117 Nighthawk stealth fighter.

Secrecy and Speculation

- The high level of secrecy surrounding Area 51 has led to widespread speculation about its true purpose. The government did not officially acknowledge the existence of the base until 2013, when the CIA declassified documents detailing its history. This long-standing secrecy has only fueled rumors and conspiracy theories about what goes on inside the facility.

Extraterrestrial Encounters

The Roswell Incident

- One of the most famous events linked to Area 51 is the Roswell Incident of 1947, when an unidentified flying object (UFO) reportedly crashed near Roswell, New Mexico. The military initially claimed it was a weather balloon, but later reports suggested that the wreckage was taken to Area 51 for analysis. This incident sparked widespread speculation that the government was hiding evidence of extraterrestrial life.

Bob Lazar's Testimony

- In 1989, physicist Bob Lazar claimed to have worked at a site near Area 51 called S-4, where he allegedly reverse-engineered alien technology. According to Lazar, the government was studying nine extraterrestrial spacecraft, and his revelations brought international attention to Area 51. While some have dismissed Lazar's claims as a hoax, others believe his story is credible and offers a glimpse into the secretive operations at the base.

Government Cover-Ups

Project Blue Book

- Project Blue Book was a series of systematic studies of UFOs conducted by the U.S. Air Force from 1952 to 1969. While the project concluded that most UFO sightings could be explained by conventional means, a small percentage remained unexplained. Critics argue that Project Blue Book was part of a larger effort to downplay and debunk credible UFO sightings, contributing to the perception of a government cover-up.

Freedom of Information Act (FOIA) Requests

- Over the years, numerous FOIA requests have been filed seeking information about Area 51 and UFO encounters. While some documents have been released, many remain classified, fueling speculation that the government is hiding critical information about extraterrestrial life. The slow and often heavily redacted responses to FOIA requests have only intensified suspicions.

Modern Developments

Pentagon UFO Programs

- In recent years, the Pentagon has admitted to funding investigations into UFO phenomena through programs like the Advanced Aerospace Threat Identification Program (AATIP). These admissions have reignited public interest in UFOs and Area 51, suggesting that the government continues to take the possibility of extraterrestrial encounters seriously.

Storm Area 51 Movement

- In 2019, a viral social media event called "Storm Area 51, They Can't Stop All of Us" encouraged people to storm the base in search of answers about extraterrestrial life. While the event was largely a joke, it highlighted the enduring fascination with Area 51 and the desire for transparency about what the government knows.

Theories and Speculations

Reverse-Engineering Alien Technology

○ One of the most persistent theories is that Area 51 is involved in the reverse-engineering of alien technology. Proponents argue that advances in stealth technology, propulsion systems, and other aerospace innovations are the result of studying extraterrestrial spacecraft. This theory suggests that the government has made significant technological breakthroughs by analyzing alien materials.

Interstellar Communication

○ Another theory posits that Area 51 serves as a hub for communication with extraterrestrial civilizations. This could involve the use of advanced radio telescopes, signal processing equipment, and other technologies to detect and interpret messages from beyond our solar system. The secrecy surrounding the base is seen as necessary to prevent public panic and maintain control over this sensitive information.

Conclusion

Area 51 remains one of the most enigmatic and controversial sites in the world. Its history of secrecy, combined with compelling testimony and ongoing government investigations, ensures that it will continue to be a focal point for conspiracy theories and speculation. Whether it is a hub for advanced military research, a repository for extraterrestrial technology, or something else entirely, the mysteries of Area 51 invite us to question what lies beyond the official narrative. As we conclude this exploration, we are reminded of the enduring allure of the unknown and the human desire to uncover hidden truths.

11

Chapter Eleven: The Moon Landing Hoax

The Apollo moon landings are considered one of humanity's greatest achievements. However, a persistent conspiracy theory claims that the moon landings were faked by NASA and the U.S. government. Proponents argue that the missions were staged to win the Space Race against the Soviet Union and that the evidence of the landings is riddled with inconsistencies. This chapter explores the origins, arguments, and rebuttals of the moon landing hoax theory, examining the cultural and psychological factors that have kept this conspiracy theory alive for decades.

Historical Context

The Space Race

- In the midst of the Cold War, the United States and the Soviet Union were locked in a technological and ideological battle known as the Space Race. The Soviet Union's early successes, such as launching the first artificial satellite, Sputnik, and sending the first human, Yuri Gagarin, into space, spurred the U.S. to make a bold declaration: landing a man on the moon and returning him safely to Earth.

Apollo Program

- The Apollo program was NASA's response to this challenge. Between 1969 and 1972, six Apollo missions successfully landed on the moon, beginning with Apollo 11 on July 20, 1969. Astronauts Neil Armstrong and Buzz Aldrin's historic first steps on the lunar surface were broadcast to millions of viewers worldwide, cementing the event as a monumental achievement.

The Birth of the Moon Landing Hoax Theory

Early Skepticism

- Skepticism about the moon landings emerged almost immediately. In 1974, Bill Kaysing, a former NASA contractor, published a book titled *We Never Went to the Moon: America's Thirty Billion Dollar Swindle*. Kaysing's book laid the groundwork for many of the arguments that would become central to the moon landing hoax theory.

Growing Popularity

- The moon landing hoax theory gained traction in the 1990s and 2000s, thanks to the rise of the internet and the spread of conspiracy theories. Television programs, documentaries, and websites dedicated to exposing the "truth" about the moon landings attracted a significant following.

Arguments and Evidence

Photographic Anomalies

- One of the most common arguments is that the photographs taken on the moon contain anomalies that suggest they were staged. These include:
  - **No Stars in the Sky:** Skeptics argue that the absence of stars in the lunar sky is suspicious. However, the bright surface of the moon and the exposure settings of the cameras made stars too faint to capture.
  - **Shadows and Lighting:** Conspiracy theorists point to the way shadows fall in different directions as evidence of studio lighting. In reality, the uneven terrain and multiple light sources, including the sun and reflected light from the lunar surface, explain these anomalies.

- **The Waving Flag:** The U.S. flag appears to wave in some images, which skeptics argue is impossible in the vacuum of space. The flag's motion is actually due to its design, which included a horizontal rod to keep it extended, and the movements caused by the astronauts planting it.

Technical Challenges

- Critics claim that the technology of the 1960s was insufficient to achieve a manned moon landing. They argue that the Van Allen radiation belts, which surround Earth, would have been lethal to astronauts. NASA and scientists have explained that the brief exposure to the radiation was within safe limits and that the spacecraft provided adequate protection.

Missing Tapes and Lost Evidence

- Some conspiracy theorists point to the loss of the original Apollo 11 telemetry data tapes as evidence of a cover-up. While it's true that the tapes were accidentally erased and reused, other forms of documentation, including photographs, rock samples, and testimonies from thousands of people involved, provide substantial evidence of the missions' authenticity.

Debunking the Hoax Theory

Expert Testimonies

- Numerous experts, including scientists, engineers, and astronauts, have debunked the moon landing hoax theory. They explain the supposed anomalies in detail and provide technical and scientific evidence supporting the authenticity of the Apollo missions.

Physical Evidence

- The moon rock samples brought back by the Apollo missions have been studied extensively by scientists worldwide. Their unique composition and properties confirm their lunar origin. Additionally, retroreflectors left on the lunar surface by the Apollo missions are still used today to measure the distance between the Earth and the moon.

Independent Verification

- Various space missions from other countries, including the Soviet Union's Luna missions and recent lunar orbiters from China, India, and Japan, have captured images of the Apollo landing sites. These images show the remains of the lunar modules, tracks left by the astronauts, and other artifacts, providing independent verification of the moon landings.

Psychological and Cultural Factors

Distrust of Authority

- The moon landing hoax theory taps into a broader distrust of government and authority. Historical events like the Watergate scandal and the Vietnam War have contributed to a sense of skepticism about official narratives.

Appeal of Conspiracy Theories

- Conspiracy theories offer simple explanations for complex

events and provide a sense of control and understanding. They often appeal to those who feel disenfranchised or distrustful of mainstream explanations.

Media Influence

- The portrayal of space travel and government cover-ups in movies, television, and literature has influenced public perception. Fictional accounts of space missions gone awry and secretive government operations have blurred the line between reality and imagination.

Conclusion

The moon landing hoax theory persists despite overwhelming evidence to the contrary. The Apollo missions represent a remarkable achievement in human history, demonstrating the power of ingenuity, cooperation, and determination. By understanding the origins and motivations behind the moon landing hoax theory, we can better appreciate the complexity of human belief and the importance of critical thinking. As we explore the mysteries and conspiracies of our world, we are reminded of the enduring power of truth and the remarkable feats that humanity can achieve.

12

Chapter Twelve: The JFK Assassination Conspiracy

JFK
FORBIDDEN
FREQUENCIES

The assassination of President John F. Kennedy on November 22, 1963, in Dallas, Texas, is one of the most analyzed and debated events in modern history. Despite the official conclusion that Lee Harvey Oswald acted alone, numerous conspiracy theories suggest otherwise. This chapter explores the various theories surrounding the assassination, the key pieces of evidence, and the enduring questions that keep the mystery alive.

The Official Account

Warren Commission Report

- In the wake of Kennedy's assassination, President Lyndon B. Johnson established the Warren Commission to investigate the murder. The Commission concluded that Lee Harvey Oswald acted alone in shooting Kennedy from the sixth floor of the Texas School Book Depository. The report, published in 1964, stated that Oswald fired three shots, one of which struck Kennedy and Governor John Connally.

Subsequent Investigations

- In 1976, the U.S. House of Representatives Select Committee on Assassinations (HSCA) reopened the investigation. The HSCA concluded that while Oswald fired the shots that killed Kennedy, there was a high probability that two gunmen were involved, suggesting a conspiracy.

Key Pieces of Evidence

The Zapruder Film

- The Zapruder film, a home movie shot by Abraham

Zapruder, captured the assassination in graphic detail. The film has been extensively analyzed frame-by-frame, providing critical visual evidence of the event. It shows the fatal headshot and has fueled debates about the number and direction of the shots.

The Magic Bullet Theory

- The "magic bullet" theory posits that a single bullet caused multiple wounds to Kennedy and Connally. Critics argue that the trajectory and damage caused by this bullet are implausible, suggesting that more than one shooter was involved.

Autopsy Reports and Photographs

- Discrepancies between the autopsy reports and photographs have raised questions about the accuracy of the official account. Some experts argue that the wounds indicate shots from different directions, supporting the idea of multiple gunmen.

Conspiracy Theories

The Grassy Knoll

- One of the most enduring theories is that a second shooter was positioned on the grassy knoll in Dealey Plaza. Witnesses reported hearing shots from that direction, and the HSCA found acoustic evidence suggesting a shot from the knoll. This theory is bolstered by the behavior of bystanders and the presence of suspicious individuals in the area.

CIA Involvement

- Some theories propose that the CIA orchestrated the assassination due to Kennedy's alleged plans to dismantle the agency or dissatisfaction with its handling of the Bay of Pigs invasion. Former CIA operatives and documents have suggested possible motives and connections, though definitive proof remains elusive.

Mafia Connections

- Another theory posits that the Mafia was involved in retaliation for the Kennedy administration's crackdown on organized crime. Connections between Jack Ruby, who killed Oswald, and Mafia figures have fueled speculation about a mob conspiracy.

Cuban and Soviet Plots

- Theories involving Cuban and Soviet involvement suggest that the assassination was a response to U.S. actions against Cuba and the Soviet Union. Oswald's connections to pro-Castro groups and his defection to the Soviet Union are often cited as evidence.

Enduring Questions

Oswald's Motives

- Despite extensive investigation, Oswald's motives remain unclear. His connections to various political groups and his personal history have been scrutinized, but no definitive explanation for his actions has emerged.

Government Transparency

- The government's handling of the investigation and the release of documents have been criticized for lacking transparency. Many documents remain classified, fueling speculation about what the government might be hiding.

Public Skepticism

- Public opinion polls consistently show that a majority of Americans believe there was a conspiracy to kill Kennedy. This widespread skepticism reflects the enduring impact of the assassination and the unanswered questions surrounding it.

Conclusion

The assassination of John F. Kennedy remains one of the most significant and controversial events in American history. Despite the official conclusions, the numerous theories and pieces of evidence suggest that the full truth may never be known. The JFK assassination continues to captivate and challenge, reminding us of the complexities and uncertainties that often surround pivotal historical events.

INTRODUCTION TO PART FIVE

The Power of Belief and the Persistence of Mystery

PART FIVE

Belief is a powerful force. It shapes our understanding of the world, guides our actions, and influences our interactions with others. In the realms of the unknown and the mysterious, belief takes on an even more profound significance. Throughout history, humanity has been captivated by the enigmatic, the unexplained, and the hidden. From ancient myths and religious doctrines to modern conspiracy theories and urban legends, the stories we tell ourselves reflect our deepest fears, hopes, and curiosities.

The Nature of Belief

Belief is not just about accepting certain truths or facts; it is an intricate web of emotions, experiences, and cultural influences. It can provide comfort in times of uncertainty, offer explanations for the inexplicable, and foster a sense of community among those who share similar views. However, belief can also lead to the rejection of evidence, the spread of misinformation, and the entrenchment of false narratives.

Why We Believe in the Unseen

Psychological Comfort

- Belief in the unseen often provides psychological comfort. It offers explanations for phenomena that science has yet to unravel and gives people a sense of control in an unpredictable world. Whether it's the belief in a higher power, the existence of extraterrestrial life, or the presence of hidden conspiracies, these convictions can help individuals make sense of their experiences and reduce anxiety.

Cultural and Social Influences

- Cultural and social influences play a significant role in shaping our beliefs. Stories passed down through generations, religious teachings, and media representations all contribute to the framework within which we interpret the world. Social interactions and community membership can reinforce these beliefs, making them integral parts of our identity.

Cognitive Biases

- Cognitive biases, such as confirmation bias and the availability heuristic, affect how we process information and form beliefs. We tend to favor information that confirms our preexisting views and give more weight to recent or emotionally charged events. These biases can lead to the persistence of beliefs even in the face of contradictory evidence.

The Role of Mystery

The Allure of the Unknown

- The unknown has a powerful allure. It beckons us to explore, question, and discover. Mysteries challenge our understanding and push the boundaries of our knowledge. They inspire curiosity and creativity, driving scientific inquiry and philosophical contemplation.

Unresolved Questions

- Many mysteries remain unresolved, from the origins of the universe to the nature of consciousness. These enduring enigmas remind us of the limits of our knowledge and the vastness of what we have yet to discover. The persistence of mystery keeps the quest for understanding alive and fuels the human spirit of exploration.

The Intersection of Belief and Mystery

Conspiracy Theories and the Search for Hidden Truths

- Conspiracy theories often arise at the intersection of belief and mystery. They offer alternative explanations for events and phenomena, appealing to those who feel distrustful of official accounts or disillusioned with societal structures. While some conspiracy theories are rooted in genuine skepticism and critical inquiry, others are based on unfounded assumptions and can lead to harmful consequences.

Esoteric Knowledge and Secret Societies

- Throughout history, secret societies and esoteric traditions have claimed to possess hidden knowledge and insights into the mysteries of existence. These groups often operate under a veil of secrecy, adding to their mystique and the allure of their teachings. Whether it's the Freemasons, the Rosicrucians, or the Illuminati, the belief in secret knowledge continues to captivate imaginations.

Embracing the Mystery

Balancing Skepticism and Open-Mindedness

- Navigating the landscape of belief and mystery requires a delicate balance between skepticism and open-mindedness. Critical thinking and evidence-based reasoning are essential tools for discerning truth from falsehood. However, maintaining an open mind allows us to entertain new ideas and consider possibilities that lie beyond our current understanding.

The Journey of Discovery

- The pursuit of knowledge and the quest to unravel mysteries is an ongoing journey. Each discovery opens new questions, and each answer reveals deeper complexities. Embracing the mystery means acknowledging that some questions may never be fully resolved, but the search itself enriches our lives and expands our horizons.

Conclusion

As we embark on Part Five of *Forbidden FREQUENCIES: Unveiling the World's Hidden Truths*, we delve into the power of belief and the persistence of mystery. We explore the psychological, cultural, and cognitive dimensions of belief, examine the allure of the unknown, and consider how mystery shapes our understanding of the world. In this final part, we reflect on the enduring quest for truth and the profound impact that belief and mystery have on our lives.

13

Chapter Thirteen: The Power of Belief in Healing and Miracles

Throughout history, belief has played a crucial role in the realm of healing and the occurrence of miracles. From ancient shamanic rituals and religious faith healings to modern placebo effects and holistic medicine, the power of belief can profoundly influence health and well-being. This chapter explores the various dimensions of belief in healing and miracles, examining historical practices, scientific studies, and personal testimonies that highlight the mysterious and often miraculous nature of belief-driven healing.

Historical Practices

Ancient Healing Rituals

- In many ancient cultures, healing was deeply intertwined with spiritual beliefs and rituals. Shamans, medicine men, and healers used a combination of herbs, chants, dances, and spiritual invocations to treat illnesses. These practices were based on the belief that health and disease were connected to the spiritual realm, and that healing required restoring balance between the physical and spiritual worlds.

Religious Faith Healing

- Religious faith healing has been a cornerstone of many spiritual traditions. From the laying on of hands in Christianity to the healing ceremonies of indigenous religions, believers have sought divine intervention to cure ailments. Sacred sites, such as Lourdes in France and the Ganges River in India, are pilgrimage destinations where countless people report experiencing miraculous healings.

Modern Perspectives

The Placebo Effect

- One of the most well-documented examples of belief influencing health is the placebo effect. In medical research, a placebo is an inert substance or treatment given to control groups. Studies consistently show that patients receiving placebos can experience real improvements in their symptoms simply because they believe they are receiving an effective treatment. This phenomenon underscores the powerful connection between mind and body.

Mind-Body Medicine

- Mind-body medicine, which includes practices such as meditation, yoga, and tai chi, emphasizes the role of mental and emotional states in physical health. Research has shown that these practices can reduce stress, improve immune function, and enhance overall well-being. Belief in the efficacy of these practices is a key component of their effectiveness.

Scientific Studies

Research on Prayer and Healing

- Numerous studies have investigated the impact of prayer on healing. While results are mixed, some research suggests that intercessory prayer (praying for others) can have positive effects on health outcomes. Critics argue that methodological issues and placebo effects may account for these findings, but the belief in the power of prayer continues to be a significant source of comfort and hope for many.

Psychoneuroimmunology

- Psychoneuroimmunology (PNI) is the study of the

interaction between psychological processes, the nervous system, and the immune system. PNI research has demonstrated that stress, emotions, and beliefs can influence immune function and susceptibility to disease. This field provides a scientific framework for understanding how belief and mental states can impact physical health.

Personal Testimonies

Miraculous Recoveries

- Stories of miraculous recoveries abound, often involving individuals who defy medical expectations. These cases frequently involve strong personal beliefs, whether in a higher power, the efficacy of a treatment, or the body's ability to heal itself. While skeptics may attribute these recoveries to misdiagnoses or spontaneous remission, the individuals involved often credit their faith and belief as the driving force behind their healing.

Holistic and Alternative Medicine

- Many people turn to holistic and alternative medicine when conventional treatments fail to provide relief. Practices such as acupuncture, herbal medicine, and homeopathy are rooted in belief systems that differ from mainstream medicine. Patients who experience positive outcomes from these treatments often emphasize the importance of their belief in the healing process.

Challenges and Controversies

Ethical Concerns

○ The power of belief in healing raises ethical concerns, particularly when it comes to placebo treatments or faith healing. While belief can have positive effects, it can also lead to false hope, delayed medical treatment, or exploitation by unscrupulous practitioners. Ensuring that patients receive evidence-based care while respecting their beliefs is a delicate balance.

Distinguishing Between Belief and Evidence

○ Distinguishing between belief-driven healing and evidence-based medicine can be challenging. While belief can enhance the efficacy of treatments, it is essential to rely on scientific evidence to determine the safety and effectiveness of medical interventions. Integrating the best of both approaches can lead to more comprehensive and compassionate care.

Conclusion

The power of belief in healing and miracles is a testament to the profound connection between mind and body. From ancient rituals and religious faith healings to modern placebo effects and mind-body medicine, belief continues to play a critical role in health and well-being. As we explore the mysterious and often miraculous nature of belief-driven healing, we are reminded of the complexity of the human experience and the potential for hope and transformation in the face of illness.

14

Throughout history, prophecies and predictions have captivated human imagination, offering glimpses into possible futures and uncovering hidden truths. From the cryptic verses of Nostradamus to the apocalyptic visions of the Book of Revelation, ancient prophecies have persisted across cultures and epochs, influencing beliefs and guiding actions. This chapter delves into some of the most enduring prophecies, examining their origins, interpretations, and the reasons behind their lasting impact.

The Nature of Prophecy

Definition and Purpose

- Prophecy involves foretelling future events or revealing divine messages, often through visions, dreams, or inspired writings. Prophets are seen as intermediaries between the divine and humanity, conveying warnings, guidance, or revelations about the future. The purpose of prophecy can range from inspiring hope and moral behavior to forewarning of impending disasters.

Common Themes

- Despite their diverse cultural contexts, many prophecies share common themes, such as the end of the world, the rise and fall of empires, natural disasters, and the coming of a messianic figure. These themes resonate with universal human concerns about the future, justice, and the fate of the world.

Notable Prophecies and Their Origins

Nostradamus

○ Michel de Nostredame, known as Nostradamus, was a 16th-century French apothecary and seer whose quatrains have been interpreted as predicting major historical events. His book *Les Prophéties*, published in 1555, contains hundreds of these four-line verses, written in a cryptic and ambiguous style. Over the centuries, interpreters have linked Nostradamus's predictions to events such as the rise of Napoleon, the World Wars, and the September 11 attacks.

The Book of Revelation

○ The final book of the New Testament, the Book of Revelation, attributed to John the Apostle, is a cornerstone of Christian eschatology. It describes a series of apocalyptic visions, including the Four Horsemen, the Antichrist, and the final battle between good and evil. These vivid and symbolic images have been the subject of extensive theological and scholarly analysis, influencing Christian thought and millenarian movements.

The Mayan Prophecies

○ The ancient Maya civilization, known for its advanced astronomical and calendrical systems, has been associated with predictions about the end of the world. The completion of the 13th baktun of the Maya Long Count calendar on December 21, 2012, was widely speculated to signify an apocalyptic event. While the date passed without incident, it sparked a global interest in Maya culture and eschatology.

The Oracle of Delphi

○ In ancient Greece, the Oracle of Delphi was a revered

source of prophetic wisdom. The Pythia, the high priestess of the Temple of Apollo, would enter a trance and deliver cryptic messages believed to be inspired by the god Apollo. These prophecies guided political and personal decisions, shaping the course of Greek history.

Interpreting Prophecies

Symbolism and Metaphor

- Prophecies are often expressed in symbolic and metaphorical language, allowing for multiple interpretations. This ambiguity can make it challenging to distinguish between literal and figurative meanings, leading to diverse and sometimes conflicting readings. For example, the "beast" in Revelation has been variously interpreted as a symbol of the Roman Empire, a future tyrant, or a broader representation of evil.

Context and Timing

- The interpretation of prophecies often depends on historical and cultural contexts. As new events unfold, prophecies may be reinterpreted to fit contemporary circumstances. This fluidity allows prophecies to maintain relevance across different eras and societies, but it also opens them to manipulation and misinterpretation.

The Impact of Prophecies

Guiding Actions and Beliefs

- Prophecies can have a profound impact on individual and collective behavior. They can inspire religious movements, motivate social change, or justify political actions. For instance, the expectation of the Second Coming of Christ has influenced Christian missionary activities and millenarian movements throughout history.

Creating Hope and Fear

- Prophecies can evoke strong emotional responses, offering hope for a better future or instilling fear of impending doom. The promise of a messianic figure or a utopian age can inspire optimism and resilience, while apocalyptic warnings can lead to anxiety and fatalism. These emotional impacts can shape public opinion and behavior in significant ways.

Modern Perspectives on Ancient Prophecies

Skepticism and Rationalism

- In the modern era, advances in science and rational thought have led to increased skepticism about the validity of prophecies. Many scholars view prophecies as products of their time, reflecting the concerns and beliefs of their authors rather than accurate predictions of future events. This skeptical perspective emphasizes critical analysis and evidence-based reasoning.

The Persistence of Belief

- Despite skepticism, belief in prophecies remains widespread. The enduring appeal of prophecies can be attributed to their ability to address fundamental human questions about fate, purpose, and the future. In times of uncertainty or crisis, prophecies can provide a sense of meaning and direction.

Conclusion

The persistence of ancient prophecies highlights the enduring power of belief and the human desire to understand the future. Whether viewed as divine revelations, historical artifacts, or cultural expressions, prophecies continue to captivate and influence people around the world. As we explore these enigmatic predictions, we are reminded of the complex interplay between faith, interpretation, and the quest for meaning. The study of prophecies invites us to reflect on our hopes and fears, our past and future, and the timeless mysteries that shape our existence.

15

Chapter Fifteen: The Influence of Secret Knowledge on Modern Science

The quest for knowledge has always driven human progress, but throughout history, certain strands of knowledge have remained hidden or obscured, only surfacing to influence the mainstream at pivotal moments. This chapter explores how esoteric and secret knowledge has shaped modern science. From the alchemical roots of chemistry to the mystical underpinnings of quantum physics, we examine the profound impact of hidden wisdom on scientific discovery and innovation.

Alchemical Foundations

Alchemy and the Birth of Chemistry

- Alchemy, with its focus on the transformation of substances, laid the groundwork for modern chemistry. Alchemists sought to transmute base metals into gold, discover the elixir of life, and understand the fundamental principles of matter. Though often dismissed as pseudoscience, alchemy's experimental techniques and theoretical insights were crucial in the development of modern scientific methods.

Key Figures and Contributions

- Figures such as Paracelsus and Robert Boyle were instrumental in bridging the gap between alchemy and chemistry. Paracelsus introduced the use of chemicals in medicine, challenging traditional medical practices, while Boyle's work on gases and the formulation of Boyle's Law were foundational to modern chemistry and physics.

Mysticism and Mathematics

Pythagorean Mysteries

- The ancient Greek philosopher Pythagoras is best known for his contributions to mathematics, but his teachings were deeply intertwined with mysticism. Pythagoras believed that numbers held the key to understanding the universe, and his mystical approach to mathematics influenced later developments in the field.

Sacred Geometry

- Sacred geometry, which explores the symbolic and spiritual significance of geometric shapes and patterns, has had a lasting impact on mathematics and architecture. The study of fractals, the Fibonacci sequence, and the golden ratio all reflect the intersection of mathematical beauty and mystical insight.

Astrology and Astronomy

From Astrology to Astronomy

- In ancient times, astrology and astronomy were closely linked. Astrologers studied the heavens to understand celestial influences on human affairs, while astronomers sought to chart the movements of celestial bodies. Over time, the scientific rigor of astronomy diverged from the interpretative art of astrology, yet the two fields share common origins.

Contributions of Astrologers

- Early astronomers like Johannes Kepler and Tycho Brahe, who made significant contributions to our understanding of planetary motion, were also practicing astrologers. Their work demonstrates how the quest to understand celestial influences on human life spurred advancements in the scientific study of the stars.

Quantum Mysticism

The Strange World of Quantum Physics

○ Quantum physics, with its counterintuitive principles and mysterious phenomena, has drawn comparisons to mystical and esoteric traditions. Concepts such as wave-particle duality, quantum entanglement, and the observer effect challenge our conventional understanding of reality and have led some physicists to explore parallels with Eastern mysticism.

The Tao of Physics

○ In his influential book *The Tao of Physics*, physicist Fritjof Capra explores the similarities between quantum physics and Eastern philosophies such as Taoism and Buddhism. Capra argues that both scientific and mystical traditions seek to understand the fundamental nature of reality, and that their insights can complement each other.

The Influence of Esoteric Societies

The Royal Society and Freemasonry

○ The Royal Society, founded in the 17th century, played a crucial role in the advancement of science during the Enlightenment. Many of its founding members were also Freemasons, whose esoteric beliefs in the pursuit of knowledge and the secrets of nature aligned with the scientific ethos of the Society.

Rosicrucianism and the Scientific Revolution

- The Rosicrucian movement, with its blend of alchemy, mysticism, and early scientific thought, influenced many key figures of the Scientific Revolution. The Rosicrucians promoted a vision of a hidden knowledge that could transform society, and their ideas helped to shape the development of modern science.

Ethical and Philosophical Implications

The Responsibility of Knowledge

- The intersection of secret knowledge and modern science raises important ethical questions. The use of scientific discoveries for both beneficial and harmful purposes highlights the need for ethical considerations in the pursuit and application of knowledge. The esoteric principle of "as above, so below" reminds us of the interconnectedness of all things and the responsibility that comes with wielding power.

The Quest for Unity

- Both science and esoteric traditions seek to uncover the underlying unity of the cosmos. This quest for a unified understanding of reality can foster a sense of wonder and humility, encouraging collaboration and the responsible use of knowledge to improve the human condition.

Conclusion

The influence of secret knowledge on modern science is a testament to the enduring quest for understanding that drives human progress.

From the alchemists' laboratories to the equations of quantum physicists, the interplay between hidden wisdom and scientific discovery has shaped our understanding of the world in profound ways. As we continue to explore the frontiers of knowledge, the lessons of the past remind us of the importance of curiosity, humility, and ethical responsibility in our pursuit of truth.

EPILOGUE

Embracing the Unknown

As we reach the end of *Forbidden FREQUENCIES: Unveiling the World's Hidden Truths*, we find ourselves standing at the threshold of the known and the unknown. The journey through the hidden realms of history, belief, and conspiracy has been as enlightening as it has been mysterious. We have delved into secret societies, explored the depths of human belief, uncovered ancient prophecies, and scrutinized modern conspiracies. Each chapter has brought us closer to understanding the intricate tapestry of hidden truths that shape our world.

The Allure of Mystery

Mystery has a unique power to captivate the human mind. It beckons us to question, to seek, and to explore. The mysteries we have encountered in these pages—from the secrets of the Vatican Archives to the enigma of Area 51—serve as reminders of the vastness of the unknown and the limits of our knowledge. Yet, it is this very uncertainty that drives us forward. The allure of mystery compels us to keep asking questions, to push the boundaries of understanding, and to embrace the journey of discovery.

The Power of Belief

Belief is a double-edged sword. It can inspire great acts of courage and creativity, but it can also lead to deception and division. Throughout history, belief in the unseen, the mystical, and the conspiratorial has shaped societies and driven human progress. The stories and theories we believe in reflect our deepest hopes, fears, and aspirations. They provide a framework through which we interpret the world and our place within it. As we have seen, belief can heal, it can harm, and it can transform.

A Call for Critical Inquiry

In our exploration of forbidden knowledge, one theme has emerged consistently: the importance of critical inquiry. The mysteries and conspiracies we have examined often blur the line between fact and fiction. Distinguishing truth from falsehood requires a careful balance of skepticism and open-mindedness. Critical inquiry demands that we question our assumptions, seek out reliable evidence, and remain vigilant against the allure of easy answers. It is through this rigorous process that we can uncover the hidden truths that lie beneath the surface.

The Journey Continues

The quest for knowledge and understanding is an ongoing journey. As we close this book, we are reminded that the search for truth is never complete. New discoveries, new theories, and new mysteries will continue to emerge, challenging us to rethink what we know and to explore what we do not. The journey through forbidden frequencies is a testament to the enduring human spirit of curiosity and the relentless pursuit of truth.

Final Reflections

As we part ways, let us carry forward the lessons learned from our exploration of the world's hidden truths. Let us remain open to the mysteries that surround us, mindful of the power of belief, and committed to the pursuit of knowledge. In the words of Socrates, "The only true wisdom is in knowing you know nothing." May this humble acknowledgment of our limitations inspire us to keep questioning, keep seeking, and keep embracing the unknown.

Thank you for joining me on this journey through the enigmatic, the forbidden, and the controversial. May the insights gained from this exploration spark new questions and inspire you to delve deeper into the mysteries that shape our world. The quest for truth is a journey without end, and the road ahead is filled with endless possibilities.

About the Author:

Demetri Welsh is a leading figure in the exploration of the metaphysical and the occult. With decades of experience as a psychic reader and energy worker, Welsh has captivated audiences worldwide with his fearless approach to unveiling hidden truths. As the host of the *Forbidden Frequencies* podcast, he delves into the darkest and most mysterious topics, bringing light to the shadows. Visit demetriwelsh.com to learn more.

Join the Conversation: Follow Demetri Welsh on Spotify and iHeartRadio for more provocative episodes of *Forbidden Frequencies*. Subscribe and share to stay connected with the latest revelations.

Dare to Unveil the Truth. Dive into the Forbidden.

Appendices

Appendix A: Recommended Reading and Resources

For those intrigued by the topics covered in *Forbidden FREQUEN-CIES: Unveiling the World's Hidden Truths*, the following resources provide further exploration and insight into the subjects of secret societies, conspiracies, esoteric knowledge, and more.

Books:

- *The Secret Teachings of All Ages* by Manly P. Hall
- *Holy Blood, Holy Grail* by Michael Baigent, Richard Leigh, and Henry Lincoln
- *The Hiram Key* by Christopher Knight and Robert Lomas
- *Rule by Secrecy* by Jim Marrs
- *The Hidden History of the Human Race* by Michael A. Cremo and Richard L. Thompson
- *The Tao of Physics* by Fritjof Capra
- *Cosmos and Psyche* by Richard Tarnas

Documentaries:

- *Ancient Aliens* (History Channel)
- *The Men Who Killed Kennedy* (History Channel)
- *Secret Societies and their Power in the 20th Century* (Lifting the Veil)

- *Out of the Blue* (James Fox)
- *Zeitgeist* (Peter Joseph)

Websites:

- The Illuminati Official Website
- The Freemasons Grand Lodge
- The Rosicrucian Order, AMORC
- Project Camelot
- The Disclosure Project

Appendix B: Glossary of Terms

Alchemy: An ancient practice combining elements of chemistry, physics, astrology, art, semiotics, metallurgy, medicine, and mysticism.

Astrology: The study of the movements and relative positions of celestial bodies interpreted as having an influence on human affairs and the natural world.

Conspiracy Theory: A theory that explains an event or set of circumstances as the result of a secret plot by usually powerful conspirators.

Esotericism: Knowledge intended for or understood by a small, specialized group, often of a spiritual or mystical nature.

Gnosis: Knowledge of spiritual mysteries; in Gnosticism, this refers to the esoteric knowledge necessary for salvation.

Illuminati: A purported secret society that is alleged to control world affairs through present-day governments and corporations.

Mysticism: The belief that union with or absorption into the Deity or the absolute, or the spiritual apprehension of knowledge inaccessible to the intellect, may be attained through contemplation and self-surrender.

Occult: Supernatural, mystical, or magical beliefs, practices, or phenomena.

Rosicrucianism: A philosophical secret society said to have been founded in late medieval Germany, holding a doctrine "built on esoteric truths of the ancient past."

Secret Society: An organization whose members are sworn to secrecy about its activities, often holding knowledge not available to the general public.

Appendix C: Author's Notes and Sources

This appendix provides detailed references and annotations for the information presented in *Forbidden FREQUENCIES: Unveiling the World's Hidden Truths*. It includes source materials, author's notes on interpretations, and additional insights into the topics covered.

Sources:

- Hall, Manly P. *The Secret Teachings of All Ages*. TarcherPerigee, 2003.
- Baigent, Michael, Leigh, Richard, and Lincoln, Henry. *Holy Blood, Holy Grail*. Dell, 2004.
- Knight, Christopher, and Lomas, Robert. *The Hiram Key*. Fair Winds Press, 2001.
- Marrs, Jim. *Rule by Secrecy*. William Morrow Paperbacks, 2001.
- Cremo, Michael A., and Thompson, Richard L. *The Hidden History of the Human Race*. Torchlight Publishing, 1999.
- Capra, Fritjof. *The Tao of Physics*. Shambhala, 2010.
- Tarnas, Richard. *Cosmos and Psyche*. Plume, 2007.

Author's Notes:

Interpretations of Historical Texts:

- The interpretations of historical and esoteric texts

presented in this book are based on extensive research and cross-referencing with multiple sources. Where interpretations differ among scholars, the most commonly accepted views have been presented, with notes on alternative perspectives.

Conspiracy Theory Analysis:

- Conspiracy theories are analyzed with a critical eye, focusing on the balance between skepticism and open-minded inquiry. The goal is to present evidence and arguments from multiple sides, allowing readers to form their own informed opinions.

Esoteric Practices:

- The descriptions of esoteric practices and beliefs are drawn from primary sources and scholarly works in the fields of religious studies, anthropology, and history. Practices are presented with respect to their cultural and historical contexts.

This comprehensive exploration of secret knowledge, hidden truths, and the power of belief aims to illuminate the mysteries that have fascinated humanity for centuries. As you delve deeper into these topics, may you find not only answers but also new questions that spark your curiosity and inspire your quest for understanding.